The Idea of Building

Other Titles Available From E & FN Spon

Design Strategies in Architecture
GH Baker

Elements of Architecture
P Von Meiss

Emerging Concepts in Urban Space Design
GH Broadbent

The Way We Build Now
A Orton

Architecture and Construction in Steel
Edited by A Blanc, M McEvoy & R Plank

Air Conditioning
DV Chadderton

Construction Methods and Planning
JR Illingworth

Illustrated Encyclopedia of Building Services
D Kut

The Idea of Building

Thought and action in the design and
production of buildings

Steven Groák

E & FN SPON

An Imprint of Chapman & Hall

London · Glasgow · New York · Tokyo · Melbourne · Madras

Published by E & FN Spon, an imprint of Chapman & Hall,
2-6 Boundary Row, London SE1 8HN, UK

Chapman & Hall, 2-6 Boundary Row, London SE1 8HN, UK

Blackie Academic & Professional, Wester Cleddens Road,
Bishopbriggs, Glasgow G64 2NZ, UK

Chapman & Hall Inc., One Penn Plaza, 41st Floor, NY 10119, USA

Chapman & Hall Japan, Thomson Publishing Japan, Hirakawacho
Nemoto Building, 6F, 1-7-11 Hirakawa-cho, Chiyoda-ku, Tokyo 102,
Japan

Chapman & Hall Australia, Thomas Nelson Australia, 102 Dodds
Street, South Melbourne, Victoria 3205, Australia

Chapman & Hall India, R. Seshadri, 32 Second Main Road, CIT East,
Madras 600 035, India

First edition 1992
Reprinted 1993

© 1992 Steven Groák

Typeset in 10/12 Palatino by Keyboard Services, Luton, Beds
Printed in Great Britain by St Edmundsbury Press,
Bury St Edmunds, Suffolk
ISBN 0 419 17830 9 (PB)

A catalogue record for this book is available from the British Library
Library of Congress Cataloging-in-Publication Data available

Contents

Acknowledgements

Copyright acknowledgements

The following illustrations are published by kind permission of the following:

The cover includes the painting 'The revolution of the viaducts' by Paul Klee, photograph by Elke Walford, Fotowerkstatt, courtesy Hamburger Kunsthalle. Figure 3 is from a Doonesbury cartoon, Universal Press Syndicate © GB Trudeau, supplied by Inter-continental Features, London. Figure 5 is by Sally and Richard Greenhill, negative number B68/34, courtesy Photographers: Photo Library, London. Figure 7 is from the Bentham Papers, folio 115/44, courtesy the Librarian of University College London. Figure 11 is by Foto-Ottica, Viareggio, Italy. Figures 21, 24, 29 are Hedrich-Blessing photographs (respectively refs: HB-13809-S6, HB-14490-E cropped, HB-18506-I3 cropped), courtesy Chicago Historical Society. Figure 28 is Photograph K7622: Mies van der Rohe, Ludwig; *Library and Administration Building, Illinois Institute of Technology*; 1944. Corner Study (southeast corner); Pencil on paper, 40×30" (101.6×76.2cm); Collection, Mies van der Rohe Archive, The Museum of Modern Art, New York. Gift of the architect. Figure 31 is courtesy the Ove Arup Partnership. Figure 34 is negative 8802-1, courtesy Studio Kalevi A. Mäkinen, Finland. Figure 44 is two drawings by Alvar Aalto, reproduced from *Architectural Review* (1936), courtesy the Museum of Finnish Architecture (ref: 43/1393 and 43/1394), Helsinki. Figure 49 is by Heikki Havas, courtesy the Museum of Finnish Architecture (ref: 49/151), Helsinki. Figure 52 is by Leonardo Mosso, courtesy the Museum of Finnish Architecture (ref: 49/46), Helsinki.

Figures 1, 2, 4, 6, 8–10, 12–20, 22–23, 25–27, 30, 32–33, 35, 37–43, 45–48, 50–51, 53 are all copyright Steven Groák, including redrawings based on evidence from several sources.

The following quotations are published by kind permission of the following: on page 133, the 12 lines from *Naming of Parts*, part of the poem, are reprinted from Henry Reed's *Collected Poems* edited by Jon Stallworthy (1991) by permission of Oxford University Press. On page 139, the quotation on the panda is from an article by Derek Ager. This first appeared in *New Scientist* magazine London, the weekly review of science and technology. 'Interlude' in *The Idea of Building* from *Invisible Cities* by Italo Calvino, © 1972 by Giulio Einaudi editore S.p.a. translated by William Weaver, © 1974 by Harcourt Brace Jovanovich, Inc., reprinted by permission of Harcourt Brace Jovanovich, Inc.

Personal acknowledgements

Any author relies enormously on many people – friends, previous teachers, other authors, colleagues. The debt may be incurred through conversations which, at the time, seemed almost incidental, or through deliberate analyses of the ideas at hand. Afterwards, it is not always easy to identify the precise origins or attributions of the ideas which inform the new work. Formal reference to books which plainly deal with particular topics is the only straightforward part of this recognition of the corporate effort. I am no exception to this dilemma. Nevertheless, I wish to place on record my gratitude to many people. If I thought it possible to get away with blaming them for the many confusions, unconvincing tales, blind alleys and plain mistakes which no doubt still inhabit my text, I should cheerfully do so. But I confess they are mine own.

First of all, I thank the sponsors of this book, The Building Centre Trust, and their Steering Committee, with whom I have worked so happily and whose advice has been of critical benefit: the Chairman, Professor Derek Sugden (long a friend and mentor); Geoffrey Ashworth; Max Fordham; John Walkerdine; Professor Douglass Wise; and John George, Director of the Trust, whose vision for the book provided a constant inspiration and whose encouragement during my illness early on was crucial to the book's momentum.

Dr William Allen very generously allowed me sight of the

typescript of two chapters of his own forthcoming book, and these helped immensely in clarifying the relationship between climate and building design and in understanding the phenomenon his practice has identified as 'thermal pumping'.

Professor Walter Kroner responded promptly to my request for reports on his recent research at Rensselaer Polytechnic Institute.

Jussi Rautsi and I have worked for some time together on studies of the Finnish architect, Alvar Aalto, and this has improved my understanding there in many ways.

I am indebted to staff at several institutions for help in finding illustrations: Pauline Borland, London; Eileen Flanagan of the Chicago Historical Society; Thomas D. Grischkowsky, Permissions Officer at the Museum of Modern Art, New York; Pauline Shirley, Ove Arup Partnership, London; Elina Standerskjöld, Curator of the Archives at the Museum of Finnish Architecture, Helsinki; the Librarian, University College London.

I thank Trevor Slydel and Nigel Whales for their excellent work on the illustrations and Hannah Turin-Oorthuys for her excellent work on the cover design.

The editorial staff at E & FN Spon have been constantly supportive in bringing this publication to fruition: Sharon Duckworth, Martin Hyndman, Jeremy Macdonald, Lorraine Schembri.

A number of friends and colleagues were kind enough to give me detailed comments in discussion, or on earlier drafts or earlier versions of the crucial ideas: Masao Ando; Professor Florian Beigel; Professor Donald Bishop; Robert Cather; Dr Stephen Drewer; Michael Edwards; Brian Fine; Dr John Foreman; David Gann; Professor Edmund Happold; Martyn Harrold; Professor David Hawk; Graham Ive; David Loe; David Lush; Linda Munday; Bev Nutt; Dr Tadj Oreszczyn; Cho Padamsee; Turlogh O'Brien; Peter Ross; and Dr Geoff Whittle.

There is less specific but equally felt gratitude to students and staff at the Bartlett School, University College London, with and on whom many of the ideas were tested in their first approximations. Four of my teachers there, two of them sadly now dead, forged much of my interest in these topics: Professor Peter Reyner Banham; Professor Robert Maxwell; Professor John Musgrove; and Professor Duccio Turin.

For discussions in developing general understandings of the issues that I now realize have been quietly simmering, apart from specific commentaries, I thank: Dr Janet Abrams; Simon Barker; Michael Bedford; Giuseppe Boscherini; Professor Peter Burberry; Barbara-Ann Campbell; Stirling Craig; Marc Hacker; Paul Jackson; Stelios Kafandaris; Dr Aida Kisanga; Professor Otto and Dr Renate Koenigsberger; Dr Frederick Krimgold; Gordon Maclaren; Stefano de Martino; Margarita Milissi; Maria Teresa Pignatelli; Almaz Rahim; Helen Rainey; the late Walter Segal; Jaimie Shorten; Ro Spankie; Peter St John; Andrew Smith; Genie Tatarian; Terence Tse; Wilfried Wang; and the late Ann Wyatt.

A more general debt for umpteen explorations, guidance, arguments and collaborations is owed to: David Dunster; Michael Hatchett; and Dr Kenneth Segar.

My late father's work as an inventor and technologist has left me not just with fond memories, but lasting passions and perceptions. My mother, my sister, Christine, and my brother, Martin, had an undoubted and energetic effect on the occasionally irreverent musings to be found here, but I cannot identify their precise contributions.

Finally, an overwhelming debt is to Liz Inman, who has borne much of the tedium of encouraging me to make the text intelligible and coherent, simply to return to the task, and who provided constant independent comment. Without that, the text would have been an utter muddle. This book is dedicated to her in gratitude.

Preface

In 1919 the Building Research Station was established as the world's first multi-discipline organisation for Building Research. Among its young and enthusiastic pioneering staff was one Robert Fitzmaurice, a Civil Engineer with a taste for architecture and music and with a highly synoptic mind. In the mid-1930s he decided that the Station had made so much progress that he could put together the first picture of the way science was changing the knowledge-base of the building industry. A widely representative discussion group was formed and in 1938 HMSO published Volume 1 of *Principles of Modern Building*.

It had an electrifying effect on such young moderns as F.R.S. Yorke, Frederick Gibberd, and Wells Coates, and on several rising stars in the construction industry. F.R. Yerbury, the founder of the Building Centre, was in Fitz's circle too – he was Fitz to all his friends – and everyone pressed him to get on with Volume 2.

But that was not to be. At the end of 1937 I had the good fortune to join him as his Personal Assistant and became involved in the early stages of the second volume, but by the end of 1938 we had to give it up as the clouds of war began to cast shadows over our work at the Station. The post war re-write of *Principles* was a worthy effort and embodied the results of almost a decade more of building research, but he was not available to participate in its writing and his imaginative touch could not be recaptured.

Perhaps *Principles* was not really to be his greatest contribution to the world of building however, for it was he who first realised that prescriptive building regulations would frustrate innovation and thereby make building research largely pointless, and it led him in 1934 to propose that they be moved in stages on to the performance basis that has now become a reality in Britain. It is a science-based concept which is gradually spreading throughout the world.

Fitz would have been fascinated by this book of Steven Groák's, conceived by The Building Centre Trust to mark its 60th Anniversary. I count myself fortunate to have had the honour to establish this link between Steven's book and his. It will also serve as something of a tribute to Fitzmaurice for the many benefits which his creative mind conferred upon all of us in the building industry which will be realised if it achieves the standing of *Principles of Modern Building*.

I think many readers are going to be grateful to The Building Centre Trust for this imaginative act of patronage linking the earliest days of building research to Steven's exploration of the contemporary explosion of architectural ideas.

Dr W.A. Allen

Foreword

William Allen's preface succinctly sets the scene in the BRS before the second world war when the seeds were sown for Fitzmaurice's *Principles of Modern Building*. Steven Groák's *The Idea of Building* is in a direct line of succession to that important book and he has also developed the most important aspects of D.A.G. Reid's thoughts about a future *Principles of Modern Building*. In D.A.G. Reid's article *A Book to Wake the Children* which he wrote in June 1973 to introduce the second revision of Fitzmaurice's *Principles of Modern Building* he made this significant observation: 'Second, there was a resentment felt by many, probably by a large majority of practising architects, at this intrusion of scientists into their world, self-appointed pundits pontificating on matters in which they had no real experience. Builders, in so far as they were aware what was going on (which was not far) felt the same. Engineers took no notice (after all, it was only building). Quantity surveyors also took little notice (it did not affect the Standard Method of Measurement).' Ironically the author was a civil engineer as was D.A.G. Reid. It was after working for a contractor and small consultant that I joined Arup in 1953 and was introduced to *The Principles of Modern Building* by Ronald (Bob) Hobbs. I soon invested in my own copy which, like most textbooks used in one's youth, was lost, stolen or strayed. I still use the Arup Library copy, which bears R.W. Hobbs' signature of original ownership on the inside fly leaf. Reid's observation of the engineer's view 'after all it was only building' was discouraged from on high within the new firm I had joined. Perhaps this was the primary reason which set it apart from other engineering practices. It could also have been the exception which proved the rule.

Principles of Modern Building was a collection of clear state-ments, beautifully written, about principles to which one con-tinuously turned. This view is confirmed by the infinite number of thumb marks on 'my' Hobbs/Arup Library copy. Fitzmaurice only covered walls, partitions and chimneys. Addicts waited eagerly for the next part which was finally published in 1961 and covered floors and roofs. It was written by many authors and somewhat of a disappointment, mainly because the committee style could never compare with that of a single author and particularly one as distinguished as Fitzmaurice. The years passed and it soon became apparent that after D.A.G. Reid's second version of 1973, BRE would not be continuing with the series.

By the 80s the subject was becoming ferociously difficult. In the 50 years since the work of the BRE and Fitzmaurice's book, the building trade had become the building industry and had then been translated into the construction industry. The craft-based building trade of the 30s had been transformed by the framed building and in the post-war period by system building, together with an enormous increase in the industrialised production of all the myriad of sophisticated parts which go to make a modern building. In addition there was the influence of the growth of engineering practices and particularly the asymptotic growth of mechanical and electrical services, together with the develop-ment of sophisticated cost planning systems. The reappraisal of contract systems with the emergence of management contract-ing, construction management and design and build, and the change from prescriptive to performance specification have been even more radical influences. All have a fundamental effect on the way buildings are designed, the parts collected together and constructed. How then could *The Principles of Modern Building* be revised against the background of a radically transformed industry?

For some while The Building Centre Trust, which is a body which truly represents all aspects of the building industry, con-sidered the idea of commissioning a person or persons to appraise the issues involved. It was John George's suggestion that a few people from the contracting industry, from practice and from teaching should meet to talk about the idea of a new *The Principles of Modern Building*. We met at Templeton College in Oxford in 1989. There were some 28 present, mainly from practice and teaching. Sadly the contracting side was very poorly represented. Perhaps this shows a significant withdrawal, on the part of the current leaders of our contracting companies, from concern with the design and construction of a building to a primary concern with management and finance.

The outcome of this excellent seminar was a universal agreement that we should commission a 'slim volume' which would act as a primer and catalyst to review many of the underlying principles of why and how we make our buildings, and in some cases perhaps question the 'holy cows' and assumptions of the industry. This primer will then be followed by regular publications on the current state of the art concerning the design and practice of the myriad elements which go to make a modern building. A small steering group nudged Steven Groák on a few occasions but were determined that it should be his book and not the work of a committee.

Groák has given us a book which is a radical approach to a new version of *The Principles of Modern Building*. He has avoided the pitfall of bringing Fitzmaurice 'up to date' and has instead concerned himself with the principles in the categories which D.A.G. Reid referred to in his 1973 article. In discussing other directions in which *The Principles of Modern Building* might go, Reid gives an example of 'total technology' which includes the 'economic, social and environmental factors involved'. He then goes on to say 'The reference to social factors suggests the need for a sociological component in the nucleus of a *Principles of Modern Building* series. He completes this chapter with the following observation. 'The problems of management are increasingly clearly seen as problems in human relations but there is great reluctance on the part of members of industry or professional practice to provide opportunities for research into these problems and on the rare occasions when such work is permitted, the publication or certainly the application of the results is likely to be discouraged.'

The Idea of Building embraces both these aspects which engaged D.A.G. Reid's thoughts on the content of a future *Principles of Modern Building*. Groák has placed buildings and the building industry firmly in this social and economic context and has laid a framework for a series of primers to emerge on every aspect of the building process and the mother of all the arts.

Derek Sugden

PRELIMINARIES

There were, altogether, about twenty-five men working there, carpenters, plumbers, plasterers, bricklayers and painters, besides several unskilled labourers . . . The air was full of the sounds of hammering and sawing, the ringing of trowels, the rattle of pails, the splashing of water brushes, and the scraping of the stripping knives used by those who were removing the old wallpaper. Besides being full of these sounds the air was heavily laden with dust and disease germs, powdered mortar, lime, plaster, and the dirt that had been accumulating within the old house for years. In brief, those employed there might be said to be living in a . . . Paradise – they had Plenty of Work.

Robert Tressell, 1914

Grim or cheerful, men and women have always made things. We rely on their practical knowledge and constant effort, both of them animated by ideas. We will continue to do so in a world increasingly busy with information and service activities.

We make buildings; and every so often we remake them as they are overtaken by time. The organization of this work forms one of the largest industrial activities in every country of the world. It provides employment for many levels of intellectual and physical expertise. Its products are amongst the most distinctive and enduring marks of our civilizations.

The everyday business of making buildings so often is presented as simply the pragmatic response to need, geography and climate. Although important, is this sufficient to explain the extraordinary differences and changes which have occurred? Or the ways in which we work today? Do we really believe that there is little to choose between the Sydney Opera House and an igloo? Or that the only difference between making a garden shed and the Pompidou Centre is an improved knowledge of structural engineering? Why are buildings so powerful as images – of poverty or wealth, of tradition or innovation, of coherences or confusions? Whether by remote or intimate sensing, we seek patterns and regularities, the driving ideas, in the remarkable profusion of buildings, building methods, building uses.

This book explores these questions. I try to show how we can discover remarkable applications of ideas, in particular 'the idea of building', and the many ways we have of thinking about buildings, for reflection or action or the transmission of our understandings and skills. I relate this to questions of language and technology, to the kinds of knowledge we have and will need as we design, make, and enjoy our buildings.

As we stumble through the paper world of the modern design office, recently populated by whirring screens, or enjoy the clear view of organized advanced technology in some modern building sites, or the comfortable rhythms of vernacular building, or huddle on a cold wind-swept scaffold, wondering about the safety of the ladder, or stand superfluous beside a modern factory production line spreading molten glass in a tidy flow, such esoteric concerns may not be the first thing that spring to mind. But they are there. Just watch how we walk.

What do we know about the behaviour of buildings? Or the deliberate ways in which people build or use them? How do we benefit from experience and greater knowledge – scientific or otherwise – as the pace of social and industrial change accelerates and we are jostled into unwitting experiment? Are today's building methods and systems an improvement on those from the past? By what means do we judge?

Are buildings so familiar or easy to understand that there is no problem to wrestle with? Do we agree with Robert Fitzmaurice's assurance: 'In some sort of way everybody in the building industry knows what are the functions of the wall'?

In what terms do we think about these questions? To begin the discussion, I first present a puzzle – about the resolution of parts and wholes – and some orthodoxies – about the dominance of assumptions of stability in the nature of building.

The whole is greater than the sum of its parts

A central puzzle in discussing buildings is how to reconcile the descriptions and assessment of the whole with the description and assessment of its constituent parts. This problem is very old, and is not restricted to the study of buildings, and has persisted. For example, in his book *All that Is Solid Melts into Air*, Marshall Berman shows how the emerging idea of 'modernity' has tangled with this issue for over 200 years.

The argument about wholes and parts goes to the heart of building design. Since the earliest surviving architectural treatises, at least in the European tradition, there have been recommended ways of achieving harmony in the design of buildings, of balancing the conflicting demands of their parts. The very idea of 'harmony' implies (even requires?) that there are separate parts to be harmonized. But many designers would insist that good design is not a compromise, that it is a resolution which somehow redefines and unifies the shards of the original problem.

As experience and study of buildings has gathered over the centuries, reinforced by the division of labour, our knowledge of the parts and our knowledge of the wholes have diverged – to the point where they appear sometimes to refer to different worlds.

This puzzle prompts many of the familiar jibes at the building industry such as complaints about the separation of design and production, or about de-skilling, or about the alarming (?) growth of sub-contracting. Behind these complaints lies some picture of the building industry being desired as a single organism, capable of overall coordination.

For instance, fundamental disagreements can arise between architects and builders, the former having specialized in spatial skills, the latter in time-management skills. Although their pursuit of separate tasks has allowed many new strategic skills to emerge, it has also meant a fragmentation of communication and the generation of diverse, even conflicting, conceptual frameworks within the building process. (We have only to ask different building owners, users, building disciplines what they mean today by the word 'functional' . . .) Many authorities assert that

3

this multiplication and fragmentation can only be resolved by the use of integrated design-and-build organizations.

The most difficult version of this debate involves the role of science and its explanations of the physical characteristics of buildings. There is a vast and increasing body of scientific information about building materials, components and specific physical behaviours of whole buildings. Designers and constructors complain that this information is available only in forms which – perhaps necessarily – are as it were too indigestible for everyday use, too general, too simple and too partial, based on repeatable experiments and measurable effects. They are pointing to a crucial character of science – its pursuit of simplicity through explanations based on reducing the physical worlds to simple, repetitive constitutents: the benchmark is in Ancient Greece – Democritus' proposal in the 5th century BC that matter consists of identical atoms.

By contrast, the technology of building deals with matters which are specific, unique, complex, sometimes known but not quantifiable. Its practitioners confront whole building projects, whole buildings – at least in new build. This presents us with the recognition that, virtually up to the 20th century, technological development in building has not often depended crucially upon science.

This, in turn, is part of a more general dilemma – of supposed fundamental differences today between the humanities and the sciences (which somehow incorporate technologies?) – which is captured by the philosopher Isaiah Berlin:

> The specific and unique *versus* the repetitive and the universal, the concrete *versus* the abstract, perpetual movement *versus* rest, the inner *versus* the outer, quality *versus* quantity, culture-bound *versus* timeless principles, mental strife and self-transformation as a permanent condition of man *versus* the possibility (and desirability) of peace, order, final harmony and the satisfaction of all rational human wishes – these are some of the aspects of the contrast.

It is therefore of great interest to note that over the last decade many scientists have been concerned again that science itself has been too preoccupied with parts and not sufficiently with wholes, that they have become too reductionist – seeking explanations in the most reduced or primitive elements of the physical world. There is a new willingness to examine holistic properties – properties of whole systems which are not manifest in the individual molecules or other 'building blocks', concepts which refer to properties which only exist in a collection of entities or objects. Do such effects come from the environment, such as the constraints on freezing rain which lead to snowflakes, to affect the behaviour or development? Are they properties of the 'building blocks' themselves?

However, this is not to pursue the idea that we require a single unifying picture, nor to discard the majestic power of the insights which have grown from the hot pursuit of microscopic properties. It is another confrontation with the problem of comprehending complexity.

Simultaneously, within many building industries, there is a new attempt to demonstrate that design and production can be fruitful ways of conducting research into building. This is partly because the conventional forms of technical research are modelled on the natural sciences. Although useful, this method is severely limited when it comes to examining the complexities of building. Designers and constructors of buildings have always dealt with complexity, and this re-emerged in Western architecture in the 1960s as an explicit issue, but somehow we have failed to find the means for combining that broad interest with the achievable ambitions of building science and building research.

A form of 'practitioner-research' is emerging, which complements the laboratory-based procedures of conventional building science and which may engage specifically with the issues of complexity in building activity. It is a technological change.

These themes run through this study. I am perplexed – but enticed and vastly entertained – by the changing problem of how we mesh, perceive, describe, adjust, redefine or operate for practical purposes the jangling mixtures of building design, building technologies, building science, building production, building use. I believe that their relationship will continue to change, but in ways which give greater priority to the making of built forms and to the services they offer.

5

Four orthodoxies of building

For many people, buildings represent a familiarity in the form of stability and continuity. This can be expressed at various levels:

- Social demand: people have always wanted much the same sort of thing from their buildings – 'firmness, commodity and delight'.
- Buildings themselves are essentially static objects, in equilibrium. They vary around the world with climate and culture, but the problems of comfort are constant. Their physical behaviour is predictable and well known over centuries. They are 'safe as houses'.
- There exists a repertory of well-tried technical solutions, which provide reliable precedents for designers and craftsmen. It is the continuity by which most building proceeds, but which also enables gradual innovation.
- The building process and, by extension, the building industry have not changed much over the centuries, relying greatly on craft skill and on-site experience, responding to client demand.

In practice, apart from changes through historical development and geographic variation, there are also many errors, omissions, smudged definitions, conflicts and fragmentations, discontinuities, failures of building programme and failures of building performance, disturbances of the supposed stable pattern. The orthodox framework of stability treats such anomalies as problems to be overcome or eliminated.

An alternative approach

I wonder about this way of thinking about buildings. Many so-called 'problems' are in fact *characteristics* of buildings or building processes, the condition of the industry, at times to be relished. Examples include the weather, the location, the materials of building. Our explanations must recognize their normal presence. In this spirit, I propose an alternative analysis in which all four of the above 'orthodoxies of stability' are questioned.

This alternative begins with science. I describe the fundamental flows of energy and matter which impinge upon buildings, and their occupants, and the consequences of these flows in terms of buildings as complex systems of reservoirs. This way of looking at things helps us to understand better the modern concerns of comfort, environmental awareness, energy efficiency, physical and biological contamination, etc.

Building processes seem best evoked in terms of various forms of endemic uncertainty which, in turn, define an essentially turbulent industrial environment. The pursuit of stability (mentioned above) is re-interpreted as 'unstable equilibrium' in building processes, requiring constant feedback to maintain control.

What is not always fully recognized is the extraordinary variety of buildings, occupations, skills and processes that now exist. As a recent building student remarked: 'If there are two million people in the British building industry, there are two million and one different jobs.' There is no mercy: we in the building industry are expected to understand them all.

It has been a problem for designers and constructors to come to terms with this variety. The usual approach has been to simplify, to filter out complications, perhaps by the use of broad strategic solutions, leaving finesse and detail to subsequent participants – such as the occupants of buildings. There have been many successful buildings and building projects over the centuries, but our strategies are wearing thin as we demand new solutions whilst retaining the best of the past. This text demonstrates that as we discover more information and ever greater complexity and, in turn (no doubt), ever more complicated legal liability, the need to rethink our approaches has become urgent.

A debt to history

This book borrows ideas, concepts. I draw on some of these concepts, for instance from 19th and 20th century physics, accidentally, directly, often tentatively, metaphorically, provisionally. For behind the explorations lurks the question of what theories we have used and/or might use. Obsolete concepts remain in partial and baffled use, all bottled spiders and scrotal relics. As the American historian Thomas Kuhn remarked: 'Scientific theories are never disproved. It is merely that their practitioners die away.'

One idea from the past resonates for me, a particular incantation. The Ancient Greek philosopher Heraclitus argued that all is flux, nothing stays still. One can never step into the same river twice.

Exclusions

In science today, the new concept of 'chaos' – Greek in its original form, but now transformed – energizes many studies of dynamic and turbulent behaviour in the physical world. It relies on descriptions which can be expressed in certain mathematical forms, often understood only through computer displays.

Chaotic behaviour is not random; it is deterministic but unpredictable. Typically, chaotic systems are highly sensitive to small differences in their starting conditions – the example of weather systems is often quoted, in which the flutter of a butterfly's wings in theory could initiate storms on another continent.

I make some brief references to chaos and to chaotic behaviour: they appear to be helpful analogies.

There is a further dimension to current discussions of buildings. It is this: we can only understand buildings properly if we place them in the context of the evolution of settlements. Cities have often been used as an image of stability and controlled change. In the early 16th century, Machiavelli, the Italian diplomat, argued that towns and cities were more effective than armies in maintaining stability and control in foreign provinces gained through invasion. Several historians have drawn attention to the importance of military concerns in urban development. This idea of the occupying power of cities continues to thrive in the late 20th century.

However, as we move towards the 21st century, the explosion of cities is astonishing, especially in the poor countries with large and increasingly urban populations. These settlements accommodate a good chunk of the world's five billion-plus people, going about their business in their separate ways. But urbanization and other changes are overwhelming the capacity of many cities for 'organic' development, for 'natural' growth. In the developing world, significant proportions of urban citizens are 'illegal', nomadic, pioneers.

In the rich countries, whose cities are apparently better endowed with infrastructure, services, administration and economic integration, other problems of urban decay continue to exasperate those who plan them as much as those who live or work in them.

Our concept of 'the city' itself is changing by force. New ideas of 'action planning' have emerged to challenge established precepts of urban stability, accelerated by the transformation of many institutions and public agencies from providers to procurers of services. There is not space here to discuss these vast transformations and the supple intricacies of their myriad development processes.

Working method

Flux and turbulence, and their contrasts with the static or steady state, underpin this way of examining the nature of building and its associated objects, artefacts, energies, materials, processes. We may have to abandon some concepts of 'equilibrium'. The text points towards the importance of ideas in the design and production of buildings, in their very making; and explores the relationships between these ideas – which are so often concerned with permanence – and the physical world – which is in constant flux. In that sense, the idea of building is the engine of this book.

To reflect on these questions, I set out in Book One to re-assess some of the assumptions – the orthodoxies – which underlie our descriptions of this extraordinary ferment of industries. Briefly. In Books Two and Three, I explore the implications of Book One in a series of self-contained essays.

I have tended to concentrate on new building works, on the industrialized economies, on recent technical and organizational developments. However, I have tried to indicate where significant differences may arise when we confront work to existing buildings, the conditions of poor countries, the continuation of long-established methods. I have also tried to highlight where I believe the impact of 'green issues' may be most profound, once the extensive research necessary has begun to take effect.

The preoccupations reflect my background working mostly in design; but in writing the book I have become acutely aware of how difficult it is to give proper weight to the processes of building. I now conclude that the written text is not the best medium; film/video is likely to be much more revealing.

This study is a personal view, a speculative commentary. It also serves as a sort of primer, an introduction to a forthcoming series of more detailed and specialized texts – by several authors – on many aspects of buildings and building processes.

I have tried to be straightforward, as well as brief. Neither footnotes nor end-notes have been provided, as it was felt that they would distract many readers. Suggestions for further reading are provided at the end of each chapter. These are sometimes my source documents; but they are also intended to point the way to research directions, studies and perceptions well beyond the space, time or knowledge available to this author.

Further reading

Barrow, J.D. (1991) *Theories of Everything*, Oxford University Press, Oxford.

Berlin, I. (1980) *Against the Current*, Selected Writings edited by H. Hardy, Viking Press, New York.

Berman, M. (1982) *All that is Solid Melts into Air*, Simon & Schuster, New York.

Biggs, M.S. (1945) *A Short History of the Building Crafts*, Oxford University Press, Oxford.

Braithwaite, D. (1981) *Building in the Blood*, Godfrey Cave, London.

Fitzmaurice, R. (1938) *Principles of Modern Building*, Vol. 1, HMSO, London.

Frampton, K. (1985) Towards a critical regionalism: six points for an architecture of resistance, in *Postmodern Culture* (ed. H. Foster), Pluto Press, London.

Harper, D. (1978) *Building: The Process and the Product*, Construction Press, Lancaster, reprinted Chartered Institute of Building, 1990.

James, J. (1981) *The Contractors of Chartres*, Madorla, Lyone, Australia.

Koenigsberger, O.H. (1964) Action planning. *Architectural Association Journal*, May.

Layzer, D. (1990) *Cosmogenesis: The Growth of Order in the Universe*, Oxford University Press, New York.

Lemer, A.C. (1992) Construction research for the 21st century. *Building Research and Information*, **20**, 1, 28–34.

Leontief, W. (1963) The structure of development. *Scientific American*, September.

Loyrette, H. (1985) *Gustave Eiffel* (trans. R. Gomme and S. Gomme), Rizzoli, New York.

Maxwell, R. (1983) The two theories of architecture. *Architectural Education*, 1, 113–24.

Penrose, R. (1989) *The Emperor's New Mind*, Oxford University Press, Oxford.

Prigogine, I. and Stengers, I. (1984) *Order Out of Chaos*, Fontana, London.

Russell, B. (1912) *The Problems of Philosophy*, Oxford University Press, Oxford.

Sorkin, M. (1991) *Exquisite Corpse. Writing on Buildings*, Verso, London.

Summerson, J. (1973) *The London Building World of the 1860s*, Thames & Hudson, London.

Tressell, R. (1965) *The Ragged Trousered Philanthropists* (1914), Panther Books, London.

Turin, D.A. (1978) Construction and development (1973), in *Essays in Memory of Duccio Turin* (eds O.H. Koenigsberger and S. Groák), Pergamon, Oxford, pp. 33–46.

Venturi, R. (1966) *Complexity and Contradiction in Architecture*, The Museum of Modern Art, New York.

Vitruvius (1960) *The Ten Books on Architecture* (1st century BC), (trans. M.H. Morgan, 1914), Dover, New York.

Whyte, L.L. (ed.) (1968) *Aspects of Form*, 2nd edn, Lund Humphries, London.

Williams, J.A. (1968) *Building and Builders*, Longman, London.

Wilson, E. (1991) *The Sphinx in the City*, Virago Press, London.

Winch, P. (1958) *The Idea of a Social Science and its Relation to Philosophy*, Routledge & Kegan Paul, London.

Wissema, J.G., Benes, J. and Diepeveen, W.P. (1982) Study of the building future. *Building Research and Practice*, September–October.

World Bank (1984) *The Construction Industry: Issues and Strategies in Developing Countries*, IBRD, Washington, DC.

Zuboff, S. (1988) *In the Age of the Smart Machine*, Basic Books, New York.

BOOK ONE

The Flight from Equilibrium

The main issues have been identified above, in Preliminaries. These are now explored in Books One, Two and Three. Unlike chess, which – in George Steiner's phrase – is formally profound but socially trivial, our means of analyzing buildings become extraordinarily complex.

The chapters in Book One set out the additional (or even alternative) frameworks I propose for the study of buildings and building processes, and the ways in which we might propose and perceive them.

CHAPTER ONE

Buildings as unstable systems in dynamic environments

It is a well-meaning act to conceive of buildings as essentially unchanging, stable, permanent, invariant, an historical record, but we must acknowledge that in reality buildings have to be understood in terms of several different timescales over which they change, in terms of moving images and ideas in flux.

Time in building affairs

First, the fabric of buildings degrades through physical and chemical change over time. Sometimes slowly, a building advances through history scrupulously obeying the laws of thermodynamics. The process will be accelerated environmentally – by induced stresses such as from gravity or wind, or by energy such as the heat of summer or ultraviolet radiation from the sun, or by water, from the sky or the ground, or by some combination of these such as frost attack on wet materials or thermal movement of structure. The ground or air may contain pollutants, such as acid rain, which intensify chemical change.

Secondly, there is ordinary wear-and-tear, the mechanical damage which arises from everyday use of a building, however carefully it may be treated. Thirdly, there is the timetable of social utility. The spatial organization and internal environment may be suitable for only a limited array of uses. Here we should distinguish between 'adaptability', taken to mean 'capable of different social uses', and 'flexibility', taken to mean 'capable of different physical arrangements'. The building's capacity for

Figure 1 1950s semi-detached house in East London, precast concrete system-built. The house on the left has been modified by its occupant.

Figure 2 1930s semi-detached(?) house in North London, modified through use.

accommodating changed uses will depend on the extent to which it is adaptable and/or flexible (Figs 1 and 2).

The fourth timescale is that of the economic life of the building. There will be a period of amortization of the original project finance. There will be a changing value on the building, partly related to land value, and its overall valuation as an asset may be subject to considerable change over time – for instance, through changes in fashion. The matter of land value, and the criticality of location in relation to economic centres, transport and communications, etc., is a vast topic in its own right.

Finally, there is everyday change in the level of internal comfort. This includes thermal, acoustic and visual comfort. Plainly, these are largely affected by the passive mediation of the fabric of the building. A heavy stone building will be slow to heat up or cool down with changes in the external temperature – this **flywheel effect** is useful in counteracting the daily fluctuations of temperature. However, in various climates we have tuned the passive effects of buildings by the addition of energy – an active constituent. This has developed historically as well, and we can chart a series of 'eras'.

Modes of energy control

At one time, we simply supplied crude energy in the form of heat from a fire, burning fossil fuel, to change the internal air temperature and to supply radiant heat and light. Later, we developed various mechanical devices, such as openable windows and doors, to compartment the spaces and give greater control of air movement. In the 19th century we developed electrical systems such as lighting and heating, and electromechanical devices such as lifts. Later, we developed combinations of these systems in the form of full air-conditioning systems. Today, we are on the brink of an era of fully integrated electronics in building systems.

Arching over these issues of different timescales is the matter which affects each building, namely the quality of design and production.

We have made four great developments in this succession of 'eras' – three of them by the end of the 19th century: the control of gravity, leading to structural forms which make the passive fabric more useful; the control of air, with its role as a carrier of water

17

vapour and heat to and fro (not forgetting the early work of Roman designers in the use of hypocausts); and the control of energy delivery to buildings, giving us the ability to direct it to ever more varied ends. Between them, these developments also define our concerns with health and safety in buildings. (In Victorian England, people were conscious of the importance of miasma.)

The fourth development is that of increasingly precise information about the actual condition of comfort in the building, and its use in determining how the building's conditions should be changed – initially through people's perceptions, later through machines. It is merging into what American academic Shoshana Zuboff has termed the **informating** of the system, in which electronic data and indicators are so pervasive that they transform the organization of work and other activities, changing the working relationships of the people concerned.

With more recent developments, including communications between the building and its surroundings, we will be able to provide local internal environments and operational facilities which are tuned more individually whilst optimizing energy costs for the building as a whole. We will have buildings capable of assessing their various local conditions according to need and desire – what have been called 'intelligent buildings' but which I prefer to call 'self-diagnosing buildings'.

We have developed the active control of buildings to compensate for some of the ways in which the building does not respond swiftly enough to dynamic external conditions. This problem of the sluggish response, this mismatch between diagnosis and treatment, can be examined further.

Dynamic responses in buildings

Edward de Bono has pointed out that the Wright brothers were able to produce the first machine to fly by designing one which 'could not' fly. The example is very instructive. Up to that time, he argues, designers had sought the aerodynamic shape which would remain stable under whatever conditions arose during flight. The Wright brothers recognized that there were too many different conditions to be met by one shape solution. They devised a system of variable geometry, using 'wing-warping' and an adjustable rudder, so that the machine could change shape to meet different conditions. The machine thus was constantly in unstable equilibrium and was constantly corrected – by adjusting wing-tips and rudder (later designers introduced the ailerons and flaps) – through feedback from its own behaviour.

We may develop a similar picture of buildings in use. It is useful to see buildings as 'unstable systems', ones which sometimes cannot respond quickly enough to their changing circumstances – whether it be internal comfort, environmental degradation, new social or economic conditions or the external climate. Without the addition of active controls, they decline further, either gradually or catastrophically. It is in this sense that we may speak of building failure.

We have therefore to examine for what portion of a building's life it is reasonable to assume the 'steady state' condition for the purposes of calculating thermal flows, etc.

In understanding comfort, perhaps we might recognize more explicitly that many do not relish an unchanging internal environment. We enjoy the slight pulsing of air currents, the moodiness of natural light, the dawn after the darkness. How far is this variability essential to perception, to well-being?

New technical developments include **intelligent materials** (e.g. which can revert to a 'remembered shape' or which can be used for phase change to control energy flows), in 'active' enclosures, in dynamically responsive structures (e.g. those with alterable centres of gravity to overcome resonant behaviour under earthquake loading). These are all examples of facets of buildings which have now to be regarded in terms of the dynamic response, under continuous feedback, of systems in unstable equilibrium.

This discussion needs to discriminate between fragmentation, dynamic equilibrium, unstable equilibrium, fractured wholes, and many systems simultaneously occupying the same time/space.

A further dimension of impermanence is to be found in so-called 'temporary works', structures which are constructed for all or part of the site assembly process, to make possible the installation of the permanent structure. Some of the most spectacular are to be found in bridge construction, but those on building sites are often impressive. On occasion, the temporary structures may be more complex to design than the permanent ones they bring into being.

A related area of work has developed in post-disaster studies, after earthquakes, etc. Search-and-rescue methods recognize that a collapsed building may nevertheless be a stable structure (at least for the next few days or weeks) and that to disturb it might endanger people trapped inside who could otherwise be rescued.

We can increasingly conceive of buildings as possessing ways of changing their 'shape', whether in visible or invisible dimensions, or as intermediate stages, to navigate through the various flows of energy and matter they encounter. Our concepts of stability and equilibrium in building must be revised.

Further reading

Angelic, M.M. (ed.) (1990) *On Architecture, the City and Technology*, Association of Collegiate Schools of Architecture (ACSA), Butterworth, London.

Architectural Review, Special issue on Architecture and climate, **CLXXXIX** (1132), June.

Betsky, A. (1990) *Violated Perfection: Architecture and the Fragmentation of the Modern*, Rizzoli, New York.

Brookes, A.J. and Grech, C. (1990) *The Building Envelope*, Butterworth Architecture, London.

Bruzeau, M. (1979) *Calder* (trans. I.M. Paris), Harry N. Abrams, New York.

van Bruggen, C. and Oldenburg, C. (1980) *Claes Oldenburg: Large-scale Projects, 1977–1980*, Rizzoli, New York.

Canetti, E. (1962) *Crowds and Power* (trans. Carol Stewart), Penguin, Harmondsworth.

Dunster, D. (1977) Critique: *Architecture and Utopia*, Architectural Design, **7**(3), 204–12.

Goldstein, B. (ed.) (1990) *Arts and Architecture: The Entenza Years*, MIT Press, Cambridge, Mass.

Meller, J. (1970) (ed.) *The Buckminster Fuller Reader*, Jonathan Cape, London.

Shakespeare, W. (ed. W.J. Craig), (1611?) *The Tempest*, in *Shakespeare: Complete Works*, Oxford University Press, Oxford.

CHAPTER TWO

Flows of matter and energy

We start with the four elements. To survive for even a few days we need air (wind) to breathe, water to drink, earth (or other secure structure) on which to stand and, in certain countries, fire (or other energy) to resist the dominance of climate over the exposed human body. Food is also needed to live for any length of time. Experiments in sensory deprivation suggest that we are better off if our senses are in operation. Employment, clothing and company help in coping with this Robinson Crusoe economy.

A person may fulfil these functions in a building, even some primitive hut, which should improve the conditions of survival. The building forms a system of barriers, filters, containers – sometimes condensers – for an enormous collection of materials and energies which affect that site, that building, that person.

Physical flows to and from a building

It is interesting to see how we might analyse the specific characteristics of buildings, in terms of matter and energy. (For the moment, the complete set of financial flows are excluded from this transactional framework.) This analysis is developed extensively, but in very general terms.

First of all, we should distinguish three kinds of physical system:

- **Open systems**, which allow flows of energy and matter to and from their domains;
- **Closed systems**, which retain all matter but allow flows of energy across their boundaries;

- **Isolated systems**, which have no flows of energy or matter across their boundaries.

Building systems have too often been considered as closed or even isolated. This has led us to treat their developments as if they could be organized without reference to the wider world. The current concern about so-called green issues is simply one example, whose full significance is still to be established. We may have to give much more attention to the possibility that buildings – as systems – comprise many overlapping systems, each being more than the sum of its parts.

In the most general formulation, taking buildings and their surroundings as open systems, we can describe buildings as affected by, receiving, filtering, storing, processing, dispatching, repelling or discarding the following physical entities:

- **People** – e.g. occupants, customers, employees, services, skills, deliveries;
- **Machines** – e.g. vehicles, production equipment, cleaning/ maintenance;
- **Information and communications** – e.g. TV, postal services, intellectual property, telecoms, newspapers;
- **Electromagnetic energy** – e.g. light, electricity, radiant heat, ultraviolet radiation from the sun, lightning, spillage from electronic equipment such as medical radiography, radon, positive ion winds, effects of external fields such as from electric railways or airport radar;
- **Kinetic energy and forces** – e.g. wind, external noise, gravity, wild noise from production equipment, floods, ground heave, earthquakes, hi-fi, hydraulic power;
- **Materials**
    gases – e.g. air, coal gas, boiler combustion fumes;
    liquids – e.g. rain, clean water supply, aerosols and other microparticles, daily milk deliveries;
    solids – e.g. food, microparticles (dust or fine fibres), solid fuel, materials for factory production, rubbish/garbage;
- **Mixtures of materials** – e.g. sewage, chemical contaminants in the soil, water aerosols containing biological contaminants, or the interaction when heat energy and water vapour diffusing separately through building materials happen to intersect in a given volume.

In principle, we could construct a 'transactional matrix' to show the inflows and outflows for buildings of different functions, although this would not reveal continuous variations over time. The matrix for a family house would be rather different from that of a factory, although they share similar concerns of environmental comfort for the occupants.

These physical flows may be wild from the external world (e.g. rain). They may be deliberate through man-made distribution systems (e.g. off-peak electricity). They may be inherent in the building itself (e.g. air conditioning, self-weight and need for structural stability). They may emanate from materials selected for the building fabric (e.g. the evaporative release of chemicals from preservative treatments). They may be necessary or unavoidable output from activity within the building (e.g. noise from machines in a factory, carbon dioxide, not to mention water – the typical Western home produces the vapour equivalent of around 20–30 litres of liquid water a day from all the functions inside the dwelling such as cooking, washing, etc.).

These flows, in addition, may be deliberately installed through small portable machines, such as electric fans, heaters, TVs, humidifiers, fire extinguishers, watering cans, ionizers, refrigerators, artificial lighting, oxy-acetylene cutters, systems of 'white noise', etc.

They may be desirable at certain times of the day (e.g. sunlight), desirable at all times (e.g. sewage disposal) or undesirable (e.g. burglars). They may be predictable (e.g. daylight, theatre audiences) or unpredictable (e.g. telephone calls). They may be repelled, partly filtered, wholly discarded or fully admitted.

The most interesting dilemma arises with certain physical phenomena which are both necessary and degrading. For example, we need oxygen from the air, but this also leads to oxidation of some materials in the building fabric. We enjoy a limited amount of ultraviolet radiation from the sun, but this will also affect plastics at the molecular level.

Logistics

In so far as these flows are deliberate, such as materials entering a factory and leaving as components, or retail distribution, carried on various forms of vehicles, they form a problem in logistics. Similarly, flows of people in and out of a transport terminal building may be studied as a problem in general traffic management. In both cases, information about these flows and the ability to communicate that information are crucial elements in their planning and control. Flows to and from a fixed site involve industrial or traffic logistics, whilst those for a moving site might involve military logistics.

The logistics for a widely distributed set of fixed sites, such as a multinational manufacturer, is a new field of specialized analysis, namely **contract logistics**, in which modern communications mean that such a network can be treated as a single system, extending over national boundaries.

These principles can be applied in three ways to the problems of building. First, there is the organization of flows around and between the building materials and building assembly industries. Building activity has moved more and more to a 'production-line' concept, with the supply chain defined from material recovery (e.g. stone quarrying) through manufacturing conversion into components. This has evolved in the professional building industry, as well as the do-it-yourself and informal sectors. It should extend into the second area: the flows to, from and around the building site. Thirdly, there are the flows to, from and around the installed building in operation.

A distinguishing feature of modern logistics is the ability to place a financial value on what is held in the reservoirs, on the basis that 'time is money'. The deliberate minimizing of these reservoirs, whilst maintaining the pressure of deliveries, is at the heart of 'just-in-time' programming – at present available in manufacturing industry but increasingly likely to affect construction as well.

However, these considerations for the time being will be useful mainly where the flows – mostly objects – are initiated by people and organizations. Buildings have to deal with the full gamut of flows from the natural world. Over the centuries, we have improved on our understanding of all flows to and from buildings, on our provision of new flows of energy and/or matter, and our means for keeping them under control.

Modes of control

By thud or whisper, dazzle, shiver, dying embers, these flows of matter or energy usually make their presence known. How are they detected? What is the response?

They have been controlled by a variety of passive building forms and, in some circumstances, the contribution of further energy. The evolution of these modes of control reflects technological developments.

For most of history, these physical flows were detected by people. At one time, we simply supplied crude energy in the form of heat from a fire, burning fossil fuel, to change the internal air temperature and to supply radiant heat and light. In disposing of the smoke, we incidentally created substantial ventilation and expelled excess water vapour. Later, we developed various mechanical devices, such as openable windows and doors, to compartment the spaces and give greater control of air movement. We also found ways to entrap air as a thermal insulant.

We introduced fluid mechanical devices in 16th-century Europe, such as flushing toilets, and a few centuries later the new systems of central heating (using water) and mechanical ventilation (using air). In the 19th century we developed electrical systems such as lighting and heating, and electromechanical devices such as lifts. By the turn of the century, we were developing combinations of these systems in the form of full air-conditioning systems – with much greater control of cooling – and, in due course, began to invent machines to detect the effects of the presence or absence of physical flows. Today, with even more sensitive monitoring devices, we are on the brink of the full integration of electronic controls, information technology and energy supply.

Systems of valves, filters and reservoirs

With combinations of these modes, we seek to control the location of physical entities in space and time. Their flow against or through the building may be controlled or modified by:

- the building **fabric**, acting as filter, screen or shield;
- direct or indirect use of **energy** (e.g. via electrical or mechanical services);

- **valves** (e.g. doors, windows, taps, pipe valves, socket outlets, circuit breakers and fuses – note that the word 'valve' originally meant a folding or double door); and/or
- **reservoirs** or **sinks**, which may be solid, liquid or gas (e.g. water tanks, larders, dustbins, compressed gas cylinders, batteries, capacitors, cellars and cupboards, night storage heaters, thermal capacity of the building fabric, the volumetric capacity of rooms to hold air at a different temperature and/or relative humidity from the outside – including plenum volumes above suspended ceilings, the air and water volumes of indoor swimming-pools). Reservoirs may also act as **conduits**.

For many countries, implicit in our use of these systems is the assumption that there exists beyond the building a set of much larger reservoirs, for both supply and disposal, upon which we can call without limit or consequence. We call it 'the environment'. Its finite capacity and fragile steady state were urgently recognized at a global level with the UN Conference on the Human Environment, in Stockholm, in 1972. The special implications for cities, towns and buildings were developed further at the UN Habitat Conference on Human Settlements, in Vancouver, in 1976.

These larger reservoirs of the environment support life. The microenvironment of a building is designed to shelter or even enhance human life; we may also introduce animal or plant life to the building interior.

However, we do not always recognize that such a microecology will inevitably attract and support many other life-forms – e.g. fungi, birds, rodents, insects, microbial life, various parasites on the intended inhabitants, etc. They may diffuse through the building's porous materials, liquid or gaseous systems. Not all interfere, but some present problems for the condition of the building (e.g. dry rot, termites); others present dangers to health (e.g. Legionella).

Form and the direction of flows

Four other concepts are important to this analysis:

- **Shape**
- **Boundaries**

- **Capacity**
- **Potential**

where these are also developed in a very general sense.

We may speak of the **shape** a building presents to the flows we have described. In the case of external wind, for instance, the air flow is deflected around the building and (depending on its shape) may induce undesirable eddies and turbulence for nearby pedestrians. We can extend the idea of building shape beyond that of its everyday, three-dimensional geometry to the way in which the building confronts the other forms of flows mentioned here. For instance, the effect of solar energy on the building depends upon the shape and absorptive 'face' it presents to that flow. The shape that we see is not necessarily the shape that we hear, or the shape that is presented to solar ultraviolet radiation.

The material properties, such as permeability to the given matter or energy, will affect the impact of flows. In effect, we must see the shape as more or less streamlined. For instance, the flow of rainwater is affected by geometrical shape, but the flows of daylight or external noise are affected by the configuration of windows and other openings. 'Shape' perhaps should be conceived in much broader terms, more than visible geometry, to sound and other 'dimensions'. We can also broaden our concepts of what it means to alter shape.

Used in this more general sense, we can understand better how the shapes of buildings have become more controllable, for instance, through the greater use of energy inputs and associated control modes, identified above, to deal with the various flows impinging upon them.

This concept should also have alternative versions: **camouflage** (the presentation of information which disguises the true shape), and **anti-shape** (the 'absence' of shape, which thus depends upon shape). Already there are systems run through the radio/tape speakers of automobiles that produce counteracting sound signals to neutralize the noise of travel. An example from another technology is the American B2 *Stealth* bomber aircraft, whose geometry, materials, etc. make it unrecognizable (invisible?) to radar. For buildings, new studies are emerging of methods to counteract disturbing energies, such as noise or even earthquake vibrations, by installing the ability to produce **anti-energy** (energy in another phase which neutralizes the incident vibrations).

It also becomes clear that the array of different reservoirs in buildings is defined by a multitude of **boundaries**. These boundaries may be the metal pipes and ducts of servicing systems; they may perhaps be the different material boundaries to damp air passages in lofts; they may also be the faces of masonry walls, where the solid material acts as reservoir for heat energy; and they may be defined by material content: timber has to have a moisture content (MC) above 20% to support fungi, so that the MC level in effect becomes a boundary to fungal action. There are also grain boundaries.

Some boundaries are opaque to one entity, but transparent or permeable to another (i.e. semi-permeable): dry rot or radon can pass through brickwork, whereas pet budgerigars cannot. Methane gas or heat energy can pass through reinforced concrete, whilst airborne sound energy is partly absorbed.

Associated with the concept of boundary is that of **capacity**, the storage contained within boundaries. For instance, at a given temperature throughout a building, the ability to store thermal energy varies according to the thermal capacity of the different materials. Stone or water will hold more than air or timber. Certain reservoir capacities are related to the phase (solid/liquid/gas) of the material concerned and to the process of phase change (e.g. the latent heat required to boil water at 100°C to steam at 100°C). Traditional construction methods have often exploited these properties – e.g. the use of stone buildings to be cool in the day and warm at night because of the slow heating/cooling cycle. A more recent example is to be found in the Lloyds' Building in London: the structural floor slabs are cooled down at night in order to soak up excess heat during the day. Current research includes studies of new, so-called 'intelligent materials' in which the phase change behaviour, and hence the energy storage capacity, can be varied according to need.

The concept of capacity should be applied both to separate reservoirs and to complete flow systems, including their channels or conduits. We can then extend the idea to include **capacity utilization** – the extent to which the capacity is 'filled'. In the case of significant under-utilization, as far as the passive fabric of the building is concerned, this merely means that the building has a very slow response to changes in matter or energy flows – e.g. its ability to return heat energy gathered daily from the sun in the cold evenings. However, in the case of electrical or mechanical systems, running the systems at levels well below their design loads can mean major inefficiencies in their behaviour.

This leads to the recognition that, on occasion, the capacity of the system may be exceeded – it may overflow or rupture. (How often should we provide for overflows?) Examples include the electrical system, for which we provide fuses or circuit-breakers, overflows to sanitary appliances such as baths, etc. That is, we do have fall-back systems to cope with these sudden disruptions. More problematic are those which cannot so easily be controlled – e.g. condensation because the vapour-carrying capacity of a volume of air is exceeded, or the spread of fire, when a local area cannot contain the explosion of energy.

We can consider the notions of 'effective shape' and 'effective capacity', the idealized form equivalent to the immediate form under study, just as we speak of 'effective column length' to bring unpinned columns into the theories which deal with fully restricted structures. Examples might include the 'effective fire load' or the 'effective volume' of a concert hall with Helmholtz resonators.

The material of a reservoir affects the rate at which it fills or empties, and the diffusion of the matter or energy passing through. In some cases, the reservoir material may suffer irreversible change through the process of passage – e.g. permanent distortions from excessive heating/cooling.

The passage from one reservoir to another, or within a reservoir, can be affected by **potentials**, **gradients** and **pressures** between different reservoirs. These potentials will induce flows. The obvious example is the heat loss from a warm building to a cold outdoors, but others are available. Because of differing temperatures and pressures between the building interior and the surrounding ground, gases such as methane may be driven into a building. Because of air pressure differences on two sides of a building, cross-ventilation may be easily achieved. Because of differences in the porous structure of materials, capillary action by water can overcome gravity and lead to rising damp. The permeability of materials and fluids affects the rate of flow, the timing of equilibrium, and may in any case be modified by different changes in the building – cyclic, ratchet or irreversible.

Many design choices, in effect, seek to control the flow of matter and/or energy within desired reservoirs in a building by the detail of shape, capacity, boundaries and potentials. In the attempt to restrict access to certain reservoirs by some entities, however, we may have created local environments which favour others. That is because, perhaps unwittingly, we have treated our buildings as closed or even as isolated systems.

Specialized environments

It is useful to note parallel work in the development of agriculture. The UK environmentalist Philip Lowe has pointed out that we have tried to create sterile environments for certain crops by using pesticides and other controls. But instead, we have actually created specialized environments in which other (sometimes undesirable) organisms have also flourished in the absence of their normal predators, boundaries or filters. We run the risk of a similar effect in the design of our buildings as we try to change the access to the reservoirs of the building by creating new boundaries or exclusions.

Current research into **clean room** technologies – such as the highly controlled chambers for experiments in genetic engineering, or assembly areas for microelectronics – and into environments for outer space (several Japanese construction firms are currently researching space stations, etc.) may encounter just this kind of problem of an overly determined environment.

The scarcity of all resources will be accentuated by changing energy economics, population growth, the search for sustainable development, etc. We are likely to use smaller reservoirs and less flushing of waste products with air or water to the external reservoirs. Just as with the larger environment, we may concentrate chemicals and organisms in the interior reservoirs, some of which do not peacefully co-exist with people and/or buildings. We may unwittingly exceed the capacities of some reservoirs, or create unexpected potentials between others. If we reduce the volumes of air (per person) capacity or the air change rate in air conditioned buildings, for example, we run the risk of an increasingly virulent built environment. This reminds us just how much we control – or attempt to control – buildings generally by the movement and distribution of air.

Non-physical flows

Brief mention should be made of three flows which cannot easily be absorbed into this framework: money, space and time. In their various ways, they all contribute to the dynamic perception of built environments. In Bertold Brecht's play, *Man is Man*, one of the characters would have us believe that you can convince someone that even a beer bottle is an elephant, if someone else will come along and say: 'I want to buy that elephant.'

In his book, *Space in Architecture*, Cornelius Van de Ven describes the ways in which 'space' has been conceived in different cultures and historical periods. He points out how space is a *property* of the physical world, not a container or environment of flows of matter and energy. He reminds us how long the idea has existed that space and solid have been understood as a unity of opposites, by quoting the Chinese philosopher, Lao Tzu, from 500 BC:

> Thirty spokes converge upon a single hub
> It is on the hole in the centre that the purpose of the axle depends.
> We make a vessel from a lump of clay
> It is the empty space within the vessel that makes it useful.
> We make doors and windows for a room.
> But it is those empty spaces that make the room habitable.
> Thus while the tangible has advantages
> It is the intangible that makes it useful.

Just as the invention (discovery?) of zero was of great significance to mathematics, so the specification of possible voids, absences and emptiness is important in the understanding of buildings and their means of production. The concept of 'float' in network analysis for scheduling building site operations is an obvious example. We speak of 'breaking a silence' as a way of materializing a finite nothingness.

An important contribution of the Modern Movement in the early 20th century was a concept of spatial flow, notably between building interiors and the exterior. Since then, some analysts, such as Amos Rapoport in the USA and Bill Hillier in the UK, have argued that the structure or organization of space in a building is one of the fundamental characteristics of a building, and have pursued its inner 'logic', its rules of combination.

Hitherto, this spatial flow has not been coalesced with physical concepts. But today we begin to understand that we might conjure physical control of space *within* space, that space can be partitioned into reservoirs – physically or intellectually, with interconnecting flows. Recent examples arise in the study of fire behaviour in large interior volumes such as in so-called 'atrium' buildings.

One method involves the identification of zones and volumes, scrutinized by infrared detectors, with local sprinklers associated with these zones: if fire breaks out in a zone, it is only that zone that is sprayed. This is a significant extension of the traditional idea of 'compartmentation' in fire engineering. Mathematical descriptions of air flow, using computational fluid dynamics (an outcrop from aeronautical engineering), have been used to show smoke dispersal patterns in very large internal spaces. Computer graphics show plainly how the smoke often stratifies, forms stable layers part-way up the space instead of flowing out through convection and the stack effect.

The problem could arise in large buildings, such as the recent Lloyds' Building in London or the new Terminal Building at Stansted Airport. The analyses are crucial in understanding what is likely to happen and in preparing accordingly. These methods further the proposition that space – and hence the gas and small particle flows we sometimes wish to control – can be related to a series of reservoirs, defined by physical non-material boundaries such as temperature, as well as by material boundaries such as brick walls.

Another unobvious, but important, spatial consideration can be found within ordinary buildings like factories. We can identify what we might call the 'maintenance duct' – the arrangement of space(s) which allows access to the building elements and machinery for maintenance, even whilst the factory is busy. This 'duct' may be discontinuous, in that doors or other elements have to be moved to allow people through, but it should form a coherent system if properly considered.

It is for discussion how far perception can be controlled by (as distinct from being affected by) the built environment. However, behaviour most certainly can be controlled – at least in a negative sense. This is clearly demonstrated by specific dimensions and by the use of stairs and doors to control space, as anyone confined to a wheelchair will attest.

Complexity and irreversibility

In their astonishing book, *Order Out of Chaos*, Belgian scientists Prigogine and Stengers show how the study of time flows in physics, chemistry and biology has to be reconsidered. They distinguish between **reversible processes** and **irreversible processes**. Reversible processes are the domain of microscopic entities, as in mechanical theories of physics – e.g. the trajectory of a projectile. Irreversible processes are the domain of macroscopic entities, of complexity. Biology and much of chemistry belong here; I find that many a good example comes from the kitchen.

We have a saying that 'you can't make an omelette without breaking eggs'. More to the point, after cooking the omelette, you cannot reverse the process by removing energy, by freezing it, hoping to be left with an uncooked mess of runny eggage.

The flows of matter and energy to and from buildings should be regarded as irreversible. We have traditionally given less formal attention to the role of time in building affairs and to the ways in which we can represent it in order to change the processes of assembly and the processes of use. By extension, similarly, our methods of representation have scarcely begun to confront the true complexity of buildings and building processes. Have we identified complexity in the most promising manner? After all, every carnivore cuisine cuts up and uses animal carcasses in a different way, according to its own definitions. The names we use for parts of the body (e.g. 'arm') are mental constructs; they do not necessarily conform to the anatomy of the nervous system, the blood circulation, etc. In the building industry we have used the idea of 'elements' mentally to carve our buildings, but it has its limits.

In passing, it is worth recalling the arguments of the American economist Herbert Simon on complex behaviour patterns. He notes that complex behaviour is assumed to be the action of a complex organism in a simple environment, where the organism and its environment form a unity. He suggests that more often it is the action of a relatively simple organism in complex environments. He illustrates his approach with the story of an ant scurrying across a sandy beach: its complex movement is a set of simple responses to complex terrain and shifting ground rather than evidence of a powerful insect mentality.

The picture presented here – of various forms of flows and reservoirs – seeks to show that the environment of buildings and building processes may be more complex than has sometimes been proposed, where that complexity is built up from simple systems. The complex behaviour of buildings may be a response in that sense to the complexity of environment. Moreover, in due course the concepts of flows of matter and energy explored here may be invoked for complex computer-based models of building behaviour, perhaps through the techniques of computational fluid dynamics (CFD), techniques mentioned above in the context of understanding the behaviour of fire in buildings, but which have much greater generality of use.

Systems and sub-systems, or systems of systems?

Many of the points raised here arise because we are becoming increasingly conscious of the totality of systems – and nesting, overlapping and conflicting systems – within buildings. At one time, only the complete building was considered a totality. The load-bearing structure, or the distribution of water around the building, or the system of rooms and other spaces which people can inhabit and use, were all regarded as sub-systems, held in some hierarchy.

With the advance of methods of building management and control, each of these sub-systems may be considered a complete system in its own right, at times having more coherence with the external infrastructure (e.g. sewers) than with the particular building. The assumption of some absolute hierarchy of systems and sub-systems in buildings appears unsatisfactory, except as a pragmatic strategy, because of the loss of the *perception* of complexity.

Remembering Picasso's dictum: 'I do not seek, I find', it may be that a critical element of design is the description – and re-description – of alternative systems by which the design development is defined. A similar point can be argued for production.

There is a school of thought which promotes concepts of **build-ability**, or **constructability** in the USA, based on the attempt to bring a greater awareness of production priorities into the design process. Despite this admirable intention, it is flawed by the implicit assumption that, for any one design, there is only one optimum production method. This does not properly recognize the extraordinary variety of production units – and their flexible combinations – in the building industry. The choice of production method should be seen as the definition of alternative sets of production systems, according to market conditions, the resources that particular constructor possesses, and so on.

As this perception clarifies, we will find more studies of the properties of complete systems which are not the aggregation of the properties of their parts, bits, components, or whatever. An obvious example from the 1980s is the emergence of building control systems for the electrical and mechanical plant of a building. Indeed, these may increasingly be linked into other systems, such as the communications network, so that local environment is controlled through the telephone dial pad. But perhaps we more readily recognize the building structure as a coherent system – many who worked on the construction of the Sydney Opera House recall the powerful impression of the structure before the building was fully enclosed.

As a related effect, we have also to consider various forms of resonance, damping and other time-dependent behaviours, with the rapid cycles which may occur in some flows of energy (e.g. sound) or matter. It is comparable to the problem of soldiers marching across a bridge and setting up a drumming vibration: they break step instead. This analysis can be put to good effect – as in the tuned mass damping systems used to counteract seismic loads or the Helmholtz resonators used in concert halls. Similarly, we find that new attention has to be given to electromagnetic compatibility, harmonics in electrical systems (which arise through disturbances of the steady-state condition of the electrical system), isolating complete building communication systems from external disruptions such as walkie-talkies, electric trains passing, radar systems, etc. Many more building systems will have to become fault-tolerant and more robust, lest they be prey to 'virus' attack or other 'parasites' or monitors.

Increasingly, moreover, we have to ask how we are reliably to install such complex systems, when the number of possible outcomes of the systems is vast: it will mean new systems simply to test and check the systems at the time of commissioning. Such testing must inevitably be associated with studies of the vulnerability of a given building to failures in part of the internal system and/or disruptions of the public supply of energy or matter on which the systems depend. And how will we calibrate these testing systems . . . ? And do we create too great a vulnerability by very high levels of integration – one down, all down? Or can we devise fail-safe responses which isolate the local breakdown?

By developing this picture of a succession of environments, sometimes at different scales, overlapping whole systems, linked by flows of matter and energy, examined through the concepts of 'shape' and 'capacity' in many 'dimensions', we can see more clearly why buildings have to be understood (amongst other things) in terms of physics, chemistry and biology. When regarded as coalitions of open systems in a real world, we can also see why these environments have to be framed in a geographical context.

Site and location

French historian Fernand Braudel has shown with great effect the benefit of placing geography as the cradle of history, creating the physical matrix of societies. For instance, the flourishing Mediterranean world of 2000 years ago was circumscribed by major mountain ranges and deserts – the Alps, the Pyrenees, the Atlas Mountains, the Sahara, the Arabian Peninsula, the Caucasus, etc. He develops an extraordinary account of how this was transformed and supplanted during the 16th century by the concept of 'Europe'.

Geography also gives us three permanent concerns of building in history: climate (with its connections to environmental comfort); physical terrain; and building materials. The physical circumstances of where we build – our sites – provide a further complexity and system of reservoirs with which those of the building interact.

The site is the factor which most defines the uniqueness of buildings. It is commonplace that buildings mostly are fixed to the ground, even if increasingly in some countries they are first manufactured in factories. This means that buildings as products and building as a process are organized quite differently to other areas of manufacturing. The building industry involves assembly, installation and service, although the units it performs these on are generated largely by manufacturing. It is a unique concoction.

The site properties which combine to define this uniqueness may be drawn from several groups of factors. We have those given by the natural world: climate; geology; topography; and flora, fauna and other organisms. We still have much to learn about their implications. We have become more systematically aware of the impact of so-called natural hazards: earthquakes; landslide; expansive soil; riverine flood; hurricane wind/storm surge; and tornado. Next, we have to consider various forms of pollution of land, water and air: chemical (e.g. from previous industries, fly-tipping); biological (e.g. from bio-degrading vegetation); and physical (e.g. disused infrastructure). Finally, there are many occupations of the site by virtue of people's previous activities: infrastructure; existing buildings and works; existing landscaping and other external treatments; administrative systems; and legal constraints.

All of these characteristics can be interpreted in terms of flows, filters and reservoirs of matter, energy and information. Several of these flows have been discussed above, in their everyday circumstances, in relation to individual buildings. Two headings may be explored further.

First, in many industrialized countries, we are rediscovering the fact that the building processes involved in work to existing buildings may be quite different from those for new buildings. This is hardly new to many people in the world, especially in rural areas of poor countries where the constant renewal of housing is part of their annual routine. For home-owners in richer countries, DIY work is a significant activity. The presence of the past provides both reference and dislocation, rather like Switzerland in war-torn Europe forcing military activity to flow around rather than through its territory – a rock in a torrent.

Secondly, in the past thirty years or so, there has been a great surge of interest in **disaster planning**, in understanding, predicting, preparing for and responding to great natural disasters. The natural hazards listed above are all examples of catastrophic surges of natural energy, in solid, liquid or gas – in land, seas/rivers or the air. They can be examined in terms of flows and reservoirs of energy, and countervailing strategies for buildings have to start with this understanding. These are the gigantic flows which exceed the local site/regional reservoir capacities and lead to monstrous transfers of energy and matter.

The very advanced techniques now available for designing

structures to resist the effects of earthquakes are a good example of how better understanding has emerged from considering basic energy transfers.

I argue therefore that the framework based on the description of fundamental flows of energy and matter – and the ways these distend, hurtle, pause, wait, accelerate – not only illuminates the behaviour of buildings, it also makes clear the relationships between the building and its site, and its wider context. A word on the latter.

Context

Everything we create has at least two narratives through which we comprehend it, two reasons for existence – 'reason' as purpose or 'reason' as cause. The first is the story of its internal coherence, the basis on which we judge it *in itself*, how we understand its purpose – aesthetic, functional, economic, etc. The second is the story of its external explanation, its causes, its reflection of the social and industrial circumstances which brought it into being, its broader meaning. (Are the two in opposition?)

Great buildings exemplify this double resonance: we admire the Parthenon, Brunelleschi's Dome in Florence, the Taj Mahal or Angkor Wat as beautiful structures; we also value their ability to symbolize whole civilizations and to imply different physical, economic and social conditions of production. We find this in less astonishing architecture too. For instance, the thatched cottage from the 1430s or the stark white pavilion from the 1930s successfully conjure some of the myriad worlds which Europe has known.

Today we react in complex ways to rural vernacular buildings from Central Africa or South-east Asia. We find them attractive to look at, whilst remembering that they often emerge from an agricultural economy based on local resources. But we also know that, as images, they represent a dilemma of rapid social change as people in poor countries flock from the countryside to their exploding cities and abandon the apparent stabilities represented by such buildings and settlements.

It is through the analysis of historic cities that we have rediscovered a further dimension of buildings at large: their context – their relationships to nearby buildings and the form of the landscape in which they are situated – be it urban, coastal, mountainous, riverside, deserted, suburban or rural. It is no surprise that people seek to conserve urban neighbourhoods, not just individual buildings. They know that an essential quality of cities has rested in the coherence of groups of buildings, spaces and infrastructure – the rich variety of people and activities forming a dynamic organism evolving within a physical fabric which changes rather more slowly. We may expect this interest to grow.

> . . . as imagination bodies forth
> The form of things unknown, the poet's pen
> Turns them to shapes, and gives to airy nothing
> A local habitation and a name.
> > *A Midsummer-Night's Dream*

Further reading

Boulding, K.E. (1956) *The Image*, University of Michigan Press, Ann Arbor, Mich.

Braudel, F. (1972) *The Mediterranean and the Mediterranean World in the Age of Philip II* (1966), Fontana, London.

Cosgrove, D. and Petts, G. (eds) (1990) *Water, Engineering and Landscape*, Belhaven Press, London.

Cowan, P. (1969) On irreversibility. *Architectural Design*, September.

Davis, I. (1983) Disasters as agents of change? Or: form follows failure, *Habitat International*, 7(5/6), 277–310; Otto Koenigsberger *Festschrift*.

Holness, M. (1992) The irresistible fluid and the immoveable rock. *New Scientist*, 21 March, 41–45.

Law, M. (1989) Fire and smoke models – their use in the design of some large buildings. *ASHRAE Transactions*, **95**, pt 2.

National Construction Materials Handling Committee (1983) *Materials Management in the Construction Industry*, Sterling, London.

Nutt, B. (1988) The strategic design of buildings, *Long Range Planning*, **21**(4), 130–40.

Prigogine, I. and Stengers, I. (1984) *Order Out of Chaos*, Fontana, London.

Simon, H.A. (1969) *The Sciences of the Artificial*, MIT Press, Cambridge, Mass.

Thomas, W.L. (ed.) (1956) *Man's Role in Changing the Face of the Earth*, University of Chicago Press, Chicago; see especially K.A. Wittfogel, The hydraulic civilisations.

Trench, R. and Hillman, E. (1984) *London under London: A Subterranean Guide*, John Murray, London.

Van de Ven, C. (1987) *Space in Architecture* (3rd edn), Van Gorcum, Netherlands.

Whittle, G. (1991) Flow-field modelling in buildings. *Building Services*, May.

Yeang, K. (1991) Designing the green skyscraper. *Habitat International*, **15**(3) (in press).

CHAPTER THREE

Uncertainty in the industrial environment

There are many things the building industry does very well, as American architect David Hawk has pointed out. It survives great variations of economic and regulatory constraint, and demonstrates constant adaptability. Many other industries begin to regard it with curiosity if not envy. It is interesting therefore to examine what gives it these characteristics.

The building industry has high material:labour cost ratios, extensive dependence upon 'product design', unusual measures of performance, great difficulty in defining – let alone measuring – normal industrial indicators such as productivity or international cost comparison, strong local influences, and dynamic organizational forms (so-called 'flat' organizations).

Descriptions of building activity have shown the dominant role of various forms of fragmentation and uncertainty. The *combinations* of these factors distinguish building from most other industrial and service activities. Five 'levels' of uncertainty can be identified, some of which building shares with most industry:

- Industrial uncertainty;
- Uncertainty for the firm (market uncertainty);
- Project uncertainty;
- Workplace uncertainty;
- Uncertainty of site organization.

Five forms of uncertainty

Industrial uncertainty refers to available resources. The building industry, as others, has to judge its responses according to the relative scarcity of material, financial, human and energy resources. There is a conventional wisdom that this industry suffers more than most from governments using it as an economic regulator, and that this has disrupted its ability to stabilize the flow and price of resources. However, the speed with which the building industry can respond – in terms of the real take-up of resources – raises a serious question as to the effectiveness of such prescriptions (if true).

Market uncertainty prevails in any business. Building production shares with only a few other capital goods industries (e.g. shipbuilding) the problem that each of the participants in the process, at a given point in time, may not know what will be the next contract, where it will be, what contract sum or duration will be involved and what technologies or resources will be involved. It is this which leads many to conclude that the building industry – and particularly its contractors – is essentially a responsive industry. To overcome this problem, firms have three strategies, sometimes conflicting, which enable them to deal with short-term survival. First, they will seek specialization, greater division of labour, niche marketing, use of catchment areas, etc. Secondly, they will seek to maximize flexibility of response to unforeseen conditions. Thirdly, they will take on more work than they can handle, in the justified expectation that some of it will evaporate. However, clients may behave in ways which try to avoid the consequences of these strategies.

Project uncertainty is that which flows from the general fragmentation of the industry, notably the separation of design and production. It has for three decades been subject to considerate analysis, based largely on a **communications model** of industrial activity. The design and production team typically assemble anew for each project (even if the organizations repeat, the chances are that the people will differ). Whereas the problems of making the building are highly **interdependent** (e.g. environmental factors cannot be divorced from external appearance), the people solving these problems work to a large extent **independently**. The conflict leads to chronic uncertainty.

As a result, there is considerable task uncertainty, disruption of learning from repetition, especially with contracts for work to existing buildings. The peculiarities of a given site, and the effects of the weather, merely provide further uncertainty in space and time.

Chasing the delays which often flow from this uncertainty has also been expressed in the phrase: 'You're on my critical path; I'm not on yours.' Or, in more jocular form: 'The sooner you fall behind, the more time you have for catching up.'

The pattern of recent decades in many countries has been to find ways of improving the links between participants; the recognition of the interdependence of problems in the building has diminished in practical terms. Modern clients have sought new project organizations to overcome this dislocation, but it may simply have transferred the problem to subcontractors.

Workplace uncertainty is a particular feature of the building site and its characteristic of a very large number of small tasks carried out in sequence. Each work gang finds its workplace defined by the previous gang and, in turn, defines that of its successor. The lack of control or prior knowledge of the exact workplace leads to an uncertainty not to be found in factory-based production lines or work groups. As more subcontractors are used by the main contractor to shed risk, they will seek strategies to reduce their own uncertainty.

Simultaneously, in many countries, especially since the 'oil crisis' of 1973 with its consequent changes in energy-conscious design and greater use of lightweight thermal insulants, site operatives have had to deal with many unfamiliar materials and products in the work which has preceded them. Many skilled craftsmen are used to checking their own work properly, but, lightheartedly, one might suggest that three rough tests are used on site to check a piece of work:

- Bang it to see if it is solid;
- Throw one's eye along to see that it is plumb, level and in line;
- See if those inspecting will accept it.

It may not be apparent to, say, an electrician running cables through a roof space that moving the thermal insulation for access will leave a cold bridge unless it is correctly replaced afterwards. Greater fragmentation of the site workforce will amplify such problems. The use of quality assurance schemes is intended to overcome this discontinuity between phases of the building process, based on ideas of 'zero defects' production from advanced manufacturing.

The last form of uncertainty is associated with workplace uncertainty and has already been introduced above. There is a great variety of building processes arising from different contractual combinations of participants. In addition, within a given contract, we find that the day-to-day organization changes, particularly on site. The means by which this is accommodated is to rely on stable peer groups of different occupations – whether architects, engineers, bricklayers, plumbers. Very often, they have evolved from medieval craft guilds and other closed groups based on a technical skill: these define training, admission to competence, standards of work, working vocabularies, etc. This network is one of the principal means by which the building industry animates its tacit and explicit knowledge, its range of know-how, what has come to be called 'intellectual property'. As the definitions of these occupations is blurred, we will rely more on the reified know-how which is implicit in machines and on resolving sub-problems within composite components produced in factories.

Turbulent environments

In combination, these forms of uncertainty are peculiar to the building industry. They are characteristics, not problems to be solved. We can describe the resulting work environment as 'turbulent'. It is turbulent for the project and for the firm and organizations are caught as to which should first be resolved. Despite this uncertainty, the industry operates in an apparently stable mode on a day-to-day basis. In this sense, we should ask whether it would be useful to analyse its behaviour in terms of the mathematical theory of Chaos.

Various organizations in the industry have devised strategies for reducing uncertainty, for coping with the turbulence they encounter, for instance:

- Restrict the conditions to which one responds (e.g. become a highly specialized organization).
- Ignore some of the linkages between the immediate tasks and their environments.

- Restrict the range of possible solutions (e.g. to a known repertory).
- Increase the organization's redundancy by providing spare capacity for conditions which only occur occasionally (e.g. become a more multi-disciplinary organization).

It is debatable whether all these strategies will survive the pressures of legal liability, consumer protection, environmental awareness, etc. now emerging as important factors in the industrial environment.

These new factors create the tendency for the turbulent building industry environment to be viewed as chaotic. That environment is deterministic but unpredictable; it is highly sensitive to the initial conditions of the process. Three crucial types of initial condition have been indicated in Book One: the social determinants of demand; the flows of matter and energy; and the context and site conditions. The combination of these conditions will be unique and it is therefore no surprise that the unravelling of the process follows a unique path.

At first sight, this catalogue of uncertainties is greatly perplexing. Yet the industry proceeds with its work in millions of workplaces all over the world. Science offers a grim reassurance in the Laws of Thermodynamics. Roughly speaking, the First Law says 'You can't win,' the Second Law says: 'You can't break even.' And the Third Law says: 'You can't get out of the game.' The task for the future is to establish better understanding of buildings and building processes which recognize the endemic qualities of this work.

Further reading

Calvert, R.E. (1986) *Introduction to Building Management*, 5th edn, George Newnes, London.

Connelly, T.J. (1960) *The Woodworkers, 1860–1960*, Amalgamated Society of Woodworkers, London.

Emery, F.E. (1969) Concepts, methods and anticipation, in *Forecasting and the Social Sciences* (ed. M. Young), Heinemann, London.

Fitchen, J. (1986) *Building Construction before Mechanisation*, MIT Press, Cambridge, Mass.

Forster, G. (1981) *Construction Site Studies*, Longman, London.

French, J.O. (1965) *Plumbers in Unity*, London.

Goldthwaite, R.A. (1980) *The Building of Renaissance Florence*, Johns Hopkins University Press, Baltimore, Md.

Hamilton, S.B. (1956) *A Note on the History of Reinforced Concrete in Building*, HMSO, London.

Harlow, P.A. (ed.) (1980–5) *The Practice of Site Management* (3 vols), Chartered Institute of Building, Ascot.

Higgin, G. and Jessop, N. (1965) *Communication in the Building Industry*, Tavistock Institute, London.

Howarth, R. (1972) *Building Craft Foremanship*, David & Charles, Newton Abbott.

Kingsford, P.W. (1973) *Builders and Building Workers*, Edward Arnold, London.

Morris, P.W.G. (1973) An organisational analysis of project management in the building industry. *Build International*, **6**.

Postgate, R. (1923) *The Builders' History*, National Federation of Building Trade Operatives, London.

Powell, C.G. (1980) *An Economic History of the British Building Industry, 1815–1979*, Architectural Press, London.

Tavistock Institute (1966) *Interdependence and Uncertainty*, Tavistock Institute, London.

Turin, D.A. (ed.) (1975) *Aspects of the Economics of Construction*, George Godwin, London; see especially B. Fine, Tendering strategy.

Winch, G. (1989) The construction firm and the construction project: a transaction cost approach. *Construction Management and Economics*, **7**, 331–45.

CHAPTER FOUR

The decline of technical precedent

I use the term 'robust technologies' to describe those methods of building tried and tested over the years and established as a repertory of stable and reliable technical precedent. They are incorporated as document, in textbooks and manufacturers' literature. They are well understood by architects, builders and craftsmen through years of use and experience. They have proved themselves relatively robust or insensitive to errors of design, manufacture, assembly or use. Current methods of education and training in the building industry assume the availability of this repertory as the core of any programme.

In addition, I define robust limits, upper and lower bounds to the performance of these robust methods, beyond which these technologies are no longer robust. Hence I use the term 'fragile technologies' to describe those methods of building which are or have become sensitive to errors of design, manufacture, assembly or use. They have moved beyond the robust limits.

Today many of our robust technologies are becoming fragile. We have pushed them to the limits of their robust use and beyond – indeed, we often do not know very much about the environments in which they can perform reliably or what are their limits. The range of robust technologies which is available in reality is not only smaller than is tacitly assumed, but is diminishing. The implication is that more and more projects will involve innovatory conditions, whether or not the designers and/or constructors intend this to be so.

To speculate further, the reason for this shift may be the failure of traditional feedback mechanisms to keep these technologies within their robust limits.

We can examine this process and its implication of declining technical precedent with a detailed example from UK practice: the cavity wall, a favourite method for the past fifty years.

The original robust method involved two skins of brick separated by a 50 mm air gap, with the inner face plastered. The air gap served as a barrier to passage of water and the overriding concern was to avoid bridging the cavity, except with metal wall ties (which incorporated a drip to prevent water crossing) or where an opening (window, door, etc.) was needed, in which case a system of damp-proof courses was necessary. All the materials involved were resilient to site use and at various stages the construction could be quickly inspected by eye for brick bond, soundness, cleanliness of the cavity (avoidance of mortar droppings), quality of workmanship, etc.

The cavity wall was robust in use and required little maintenance. Moreover, water vapour – a general source of building problems (especially in the UK climate) – could permeate through the construction, as it was not impervious. The outer skin of brick dried out through drainage and through evaporation accelerated by wind, sun and heat loss from the interior.

The method had two limitations: it was not appropriate for very exposed sites with high rainfall (the outer skin would oversaturate); its thermal performance did not match up to increasing performance demands as we changed our habits of building use and sought energy efficiencies in the wake of the 1973 OPEC 'crisis'. (The grim realities of the region in the late 1980s and into the 1990s raise further questions of this kind.)

Today the cavity wall is a very different assembly. We retain two skins, but the inner skin is now made of concrete blockwork, initially to speed up construction. The plaster may be lightweight. But, most critically, we now insert a light insulant (e.g. 50 mm fibreglass) in the cavity to improve overall thermal performance. This is sometimes used to fill the cavity completely.

Three problems follow immediately. First, with the more complex assembly, it is more difficult to detail openings and other changes in wall geometry. Secondly, the assembly is more difficult to inspect on site as work proceeds. Thirdly, we have fundamentally changed the behaviour of the assembly in respect of thermal and vapour flows.

The outer skin is now hotter in summer (less heat transferred to the interior). It is also colder (less heat from the interior) and thus wetter in winter. The net effect is to leave the outer skin more prone to frost attack and thermal movement, which means specifying the brick and mortar much more carefully. These problems can be overcome, but we have made the whole method essentially more sensitive to error, a more fragile technology in its industrial context. We have also fallen into a nominalist trap: by using the same name – 'cavity wall' – we have assumed that we will continue to reap all of the virtues associated with that name.

A further complication arises with the 1980s fashion for using visual characteristics in cavity brickwork which are usually associated with solid brick walls. Examples include arched windows and other elaborations of openings. The effect is to require extraordinary metal support systems behind the facing brickwork – again, greatly complicating what was once a straightforward method of building. Other examples of well-established methods becoming sensitive include metal sheet roofs to large industrial sheds and lead roofing to churches.

Part of the problem may be in our expectations. We appear to have reached a position where we believe that conventional methods (including traditional ones) are robust and that innovatory methods are sensitive and prone to failure. The question has to be asked: are we moving to a situation where our conventional methods are more fragile but our innovatory methods – based on much intellectual transfer from advanced manufacturing – are becoming more robust?

These problems arise because of a breakdown in the previous historical feedback system, by which both the method and the practice were kept in a steady state.

The overriding concern must be that we can envisage further decline in the available reliable technical precedents, in particular, in those methods we had previously thought to be robust and stable. Here, too, assumptions of stable equilibrium have to be modified into a more dynamic description of building behaviour.

Further reading

Groák, S. (1990) The decline of robust technologies in the building industry, *Building Research and Practice*, **18**(3), 162–8.
Architects' Journal (1986) 9 April, 16 April, 7 May.
Levi, B. (1986), *The Wrench* (1978) (trans. W. Weaver), Simon & Schuster, New York.

CHAPTER FIVE

The social demand for buildings

Do we know what we want from our buildings? To what extent can their design be based upon definable need? In a sense, every new building is a prototype; every modified building is a recognition that its owner wants something different. Does this mean that we are constantly 'mending something which ain't broke'? Did this variety result from the simple statement of repetitive demand? If not, should it do so?

Buildings are made and remade everywhere, all the time. Building sites appear on almost every street corner. These processes are very thoroughly scrutinized and documented. In some countries millions of citizens are involved in part-time construction. One way or another, we should know this work rather well.

Although most of us – particularly those in temperate and cold climates – spend an increasing proportion of our time inside or near buildings, many people rarely understand them in their totality. Equally, they have only a limited understanding of the ways in which buildings are designed and produced by that cheerfully productive – on occasion somewhat shambling – but nevertheless hardy perennial we know as 'the building industry'. Some of the reasons are not hard to discover.

Few people will be significant clients of the building industry more than once in a lifetime. Those working on building sites often see in detail only a repeated fragment of many buildings. Those in component manufacturing know mostly about their own particular products. People in design or management offices receive little information about the ways in which their designs and productions have performed because, unlike consumption goods of modern mass production, the full range of qualities and problems may not become apparent for years, especially when we recognize how differently two otherwise similar buildings may behave when placed in differing contexts.

We have not devised satisfactory monitoring and evaluation methods for whole buildings in service over time. It is another

Figure 3   Doonesbury. Universal Press Syndicate © G.B. Trudeau.

example of how we have not married our interest in the whole building, in its complexity, with the analytical techniques we have developed from building science.

In past centuries this did not appear to matter, as sufficient knowledge of building behaviour was gained over long periods in which methods remained fairly stable and piecemeal improvements could be tested. This affable method of historical patience – and its associated reliance on precedent – is no longer adequate for today's social, economic and technical change and the consequent rapid onslaught of new demands upon both new and existing buildings. Attempts to develop a more explicitly scientific basis for innovation in buildings have also run into difficulty. We must now also allow for much higher expectations in many countries in the decades since the Second World War.

Central to these issues is the question of the social demand for buildings, and the ways in which people express this, even if as with the Doonesbury cartoon (Fig. 3) it is in the rhetoric of plain language.

Effective demand

At first sight, nothing could be more straightforward than for a person, or group of people, to state their building requirements and for this to be delivered by the building industry. The aggregation of all these requirements across a country forms the 'potential demand'; it is then the 'effective demand' which is actually placed upon that industry. However, the matter turns out to be rather complex.

First of all, it is not always clear exactly who is stating requirements. The community interest is expressed through systems of planning and building control: the former considers the nature, location and appearance of the building; the latter ensures health, safety and sound construction. At least, for major works.

There may be a distinction between the client (who formally commissions the building) and the users (who live or work there). If another, such as a bank, provided the finance, they too may have views about the desirable features of the building. These participants in the process are all likely to change (and anyway to change their requirements) within the lifetime of the building. Yet they have to state their wants and needs at a moment in time.

Secondly, participants may have very different ways of expressing their desires, even if *in principle* they agree on what is wanted. This is partly because of the general lack of understanding about buildings already indicated. Many will express what they wish for the future in terms of what they know from the past, rather like generals who prepare to fight the next war with the methods of the last. The immediate difficulty is that each participant has a different past, even if they pursue a common future. This can be the beginning of a potent dialogue.

Thirdly, when faced with the choice, different people have different preoccupations with what a building should be. Some will suggest forms and images, an explicit concern with symbolic content. Some will indicate preferred methods of construction. Some will conjure the internal experience they seek. Some will be dominated by budget necessities, or the financing of what will usually be a major investment. Some will wish to create a monument. Some will specify in great detail what spaces and activities should be incorporated, and in what relationships, perhaps because they are amongst that minority of clients who have commissioned several successive buildings.

Some will be greatly concerned about the timing of the building process, perhaps because they need a new industrial building by a particular date. Some will seek principally to describe the eventual quality performance-in-use over time of the building or parts of the building. Some will be driven by political circumstances, such as the pressures in Britain for housing after each of the world wars, for which the efficiencies of manufacturing industry were to offer a new approach.

The unavoidable conclusion is that different clients will have different priorities for accomplishing even apparently similar buildings, and will express those views in many different ways. Although there are many instances in the building industry where significant repetition occurs, such as in prefabricated industrial buildings, it is not surprising that over the years many have found solace in the prescription 'firmness, commodity and delight' as the clear account of what a building should incorporate, leaving it to experienced designers and builders to interpret this within the tacit assumptions of a supposedly shared culture.

It is with these tacit assumptions that we find the greatest ambivalence about 'straightforwardness' in buildings. There is good evidence from many countries around the world that, when

social factors (such as organizational hierarchy or religious significance) conflict with pragmatic factors (such as comfort or prac-
ticality of use), social factors almost invariably prevail. So-called
'vernacular buildings' – often made anonymously – provide an
interesting point of reference.

Vernacular buildings are frequently cited as examples of
methods which are technically sound and well proven, environmentally comfortable, sensitive to their surroundings and well
understood by the public at large. They may also be prized
because, it would seem, to their occupants and users they are an
appropriate representation of their society and their own position
within it – reinforced by historical familiarity, perhaps nostalgic-
ally. Should we perhaps worry that people notice comfort most
usually when other 'dimensions' of their expectations about
buildings are flouted? Do we adequately understand how the
concepts of 'acceptable change' themselves evolve?

In practice, comfort may be less critical to the users of vernacular architecture; and in any case is itself a socially bound
concept. To recognize the phenomenon we need only consider
the discomfort tolerated by some people living in buildings of
historical interest. A sadder example is to be found in developing countries, who can ill-afford the waste of resources, when
dwellings of great inappropriateness to the climate (and culture?)
are preferred because they represent an advancement of social
status. But this is not to argue that the occupants are somehow
'wrong'. One person's palace is another person's slum.

Yet, we still wish to devise new buildings for new uses,
and new ways of recasting existing buildings. We still wish
to utilize the increasing body of technical knowledge and historical understanding about buildings and about the ways in
which people respond to buildings. Vernacular tradition is at
a loss when asked to respond to fundamentally new building
circumstances. To parody: should nuclear power stations have
pitched roofs?

To build – speculatively or for a given purpose – means the
creation of an economic asset, whether or not that was the prime
motive. The large shift of resources and the long lifetime of this
asset, and the costs of sustaining the building over a period, have
meant the development of a set of large industries and complex
financing methods. Their coherent management is only now
beginning to be understood.

Today many circumstances combine to make this process of building definition even more speculative:

- Demographic changes (e.g. longer lives, urbanization world-wide);
- Changes in the location and nature of the workplace;
- Changes in access to communications;
- Changes in the organizational structures of industry and commerce;
- A greater awareness of the environmental and energy impact of buildings and associated processes;
- An increasing amount of consumer protection legislation, diminishing the significance of the traditional commercial warning 'let the buyer beware'.

These various comments highlight just how indefinite is our ability to state clearly what we wish our buildings to achieve, especially when they represent a change in our location, our well-being, our aspirations. The social demand for buildings is poised between the repetition or acknowledgement of something familiar – but not properly understood – and innovation, something not yet known. More than incomplete, the condition approaches that dilemma of ambiguity which Vivaldi, working in another medium, that of musical composition, termed *The Reconciliation of Harmony and Invention*, the set of twelve concertos which appropriately enough includes *The Four Seasons*.

This ambiguity can be the source of extraordinary richness and complexity, as designers and constructors stretch their ideas and abilities in the pursuit of its solution, but it also provides an endemic uncertainty which resonates throughout the building process, through the interrogations of the brief and into the multiplicities of occupation.

Further reading

Boudon, P. (1972) *Lived-in Architecture* (1969) (trans. G. Onn), Lund Humphries, London.

Duffy, F. (1992) *The Changing Workplace*. Phaidon, London.

Forty, A. (1986) *Objects of Desire: Design and Society, 1750–1980*, Thames & Hudson, London.

Harvey, J. (1975) *Medieval Craftsmen*, Batsford, London.

King, A.D. (ed.) (1980) *Building and Society*, Routledge and Kegan Paul, London.

Olson, R. and Kurent, H. (1988) *Vision 2000: Trends Shaping Architecture's Future*, American Institute of Architects, Washington, DC, May.

Rapoport, A. (1969) *House Form and Culture*, Prentice-Hall, Englewood Cliffs, NJ.

The Segal method. *Architects' Journal*, 5 November 1986.

Stedman-Jones, G. (1971) *Outcast London*, Oxford University Press, Oxford.

Wagner, R. (1975) *The Invention of Culture*, Prentice-Hall, Englewood-Cliffs, NJ.

World Commission on Environment and Development (1987) *Our Common Future* (Brundtland Report), Oxford University Press, Oxford.

INTERLUDE

Thin Cities 4

The city of Sophronia is made up of two half cities. In one there is the great roller-coaster with its steel humps, the carousel with its chain spokes, the Ferris wheel of spinning cages, the death-ride with crouching motor-cyclists, the big top with the clump of trapezes hanging in the middle. The other half-city is of stone and marble and cement, with the bank, the factories, the palaces, the slaughterhouse, the school, and all the rest. One of the half-cities is permanent, the other is temporary, and when the period of its sojourn is over, they uproot it, dismantle it, and take it off, transplanting it to the vacant lots of another half-city.

And so every year the day comes when the workmen remove the marble pediments, lower the stone walls, the cement pylons, take down the Ministry, the monument, the docks, the petroleum refinery, the hospital, load them on trailers, to follow from stand to stand their annual itinerary. Here remains the half-Sophronia of the shooting-galleries and the carousels, the shout suspended from the cart of the headlong roller-coaster, and it begins to count the months and days it must wait before the caravan returns and a complete life can begin again.

from Invisible Cities,
Italo Calvino, 1972;
translated, William Weaver, 1974

SOME POLEMICAL REMARKS

From time to time, in the building industry we encounter the attempt to define some constructions as 'architecture', as opposed to others called 'buildings'. This is often carried over to characterize the people concerned, beyond the meanings of professional/ technical qualifications. The distinction has emerged over time, with the rise of the professions, but at times achieved special ferocity in Britain. For example, in 1749, Lord Chesterfield could write to his son:

> You may soon be acquainted with the considerable parts of Civil Architecture; and for the minute and mechanical parts of it, leave them to masons, bricklayers, and Lord Burlington; who has, to a certain degree, lessened himself by knowing them too well.

The English writer John Ruskin wrote, in 1854, that: 'No person who is not a great sculptor or painter *can* be an *architect*. If he is not a sculptor or a painter, he can only be a *builder*'. Later, in his book *The Seven Lamps of Architecture* (1886 edition), he wrote: 'It is very necessary, in the outset of all inquiry, to distinguish carefully between Architecture and Building.' This is footnoted: 'It is the addition of the mental *arche* [the ancient Greek root word, referring to 'beginning'] . . . which separates architecture from a wasp's nest, a rat hole, or a railway station.'

A century or so later, working in England, the German historian Nikolaus Pevsner began his book *An Outline of European Architecture*, of 1943, with the assertion that:

A bicycle shed is a building; but Lincoln Cathedral is a piece of architecture. Nearly everything that encloses space on a scale sufficient for a human being to move in is a building; the term architecture applies only to buildings designed with a view to aesthetic appeal.

Leaving aside the question of how one can tell, when viewing a building, whether or not it was designed with a view to 'aesthetic appeal', or what 'aesthetic' means here, and leaving aside also the question of whether it was *built* with a view to 'aesthetic appeal' (even if not *designed* with that intention), why persist with this distinction?

I believe it is a weary effort to classify some people as 'creative' and thus superior to others. It is the same as the preoccupation of those who find great significance in supposed intellectual differences (genetic perhaps?) between those working in the sciences and those working in the arts or humanities. (The putting in their place of 'technologists' fluctuates, according to whether the category is thought to include craftsmen and craftswomen such as jewellers, glass-blowers, etc., as opposed to the engineers who design spacecraft or nuclear power stations.)

The converse position is equally vacuous – that is, the attempt to disparage designers as merely self-indulgent, deliberately perverse, uninterested in the practical benefit to the users of what they have designed or the most effective way of making them. Such accusations are usually made by those who have never tried to design, let alone have mastered this powerful – and increasingly complex – skill.

These chidings attempt a moral distinction between 'white-collar' and 'blue-collar' workers, between those who, as it were, work principally with their minds and those who work principally with their hands, between thinkers and makers. It is meaningless, and tiresome. The building industry involves people who mostly work with both.

My own experience has been that creativity can exist in all forms of work; and conversely, it is not invariably found in any one type of work. Architects, engineers and other designers may display considerable understanding of building production – or none; building contractors, craftsmen, site operatives may in reality make design decisions throughout the production process – sometimes hopelessly or infuriatingly, sometimes to great effect. And some people do both anyway.

On the whole, one expects to find greater design expertise amongst those who have had that specialized education, training and experience, just as one would expect to find greater understanding of production issues amongst those who have specialized accordingly. No surprises here. But the difference between design and production – or between the respective practitioners – is surely not one of moral value or societal significance: to pursue the distinction is to lack respect for other people's work. It does not even produce any analysis which furthers the cause of good building (noun or verb), or good architecture; which enhances the education and training of those involved; which enables the owners and occupants of buildings to benefit; or which is remotely interesting. It certainly does not make the production of buildings more fun.

For me, the important discussions rest elsewhere, summarized in an early experience as a young engineer, on my second visit to a building site. The contract was for an art college in Kent, in southern England. I had detailed the reinforced concrete frame structure for the small library, near the new college. The architect was very excited about concrete as a material and exploited it with great skill in an elegant design.

The principal structural engineer and I arrived on site during the morning tea-break, just after an April rainstorm. I went to look at the work whilst he went to the site hut to organize tea (in enamel mugs then) and bacon sandwiches for us. The library was in a clearing amongst some large rhododendron bushes. The site operatives had cast the foundations and the first column, which was nine inches square and about ten feet high, in fair-faced board-marked *in situ* reinforced concrete which had just been struck. (The contractor wanted the architect and the engineer to approve the quality of the finish before proceeding, to agree a standard.)

I walked around this column as if it were a totem pole, looking and touching it: it was the first time I had seen something built from drawings of mine, although I soon discovered that the steelfixers had altered some details to ease the concrete pour. The site staff were much amused at my naïvety and the site agent spent a long time with me discussing details and finishes, subjects to which he was greatly devoted.

I was intrigued to discover how many different people in the building industry not only had expert knowledge, displayed in various ways and with extraordinary vocabularies, but also took interest in the knowledge and intentions of others. Not always, but sufficiently for regular discussion. Even if some of the comments were backhanded compliments, to say the least. As one finds it . . . beyond thought, word and deed in the design, production and use of buildings is the issue of **whose** thought, word or deed.

To this day, the combined background smells of cooking bacon, wet rhododendrons, dyeline prints and the protein smell of fresh concrete remain for me an indelible memory, a compound reference for the process of building and its satisfactions.

BOOK TWO

Building Knowledge and Building Experience

Book Two develops the issues presented in the Preliminaries and Book One, in a series of essays which – in some measure – stand alone. In certain cases, similar topics are explored in different places, in different ways. The intention is to offer commentaries and clarifications based on the alternative proposals developed in Book One.

What kinds of knowledge are gained as feedback from building use or people's experience? How can they be used by designers and constructors? What do we mean by 'feedback' when the process is so ambiguous?

Can we find the common ground between architectural criticism and building science, within 'building' as a noun and 'building' as a verb? Will we attend more to what a building *does* and less to what it *is*? Remember the maxim of the apocryphal hardware store: 'Our customers want 10mm holes, not 10mm drills.'

BOOK TWO

Building Knowledge and Building Experience

CHAPTER ONE

Historical concepts of building science

The array of explicit knowledge about buildings is vast. It includes the work of historians of art and architecture. It is embedded in myriad textbooks and primers for the different occupations in the building industry. It is contained in research reports, building appraisals, surveyors' reports, mandatory standards and codes of practice, do-it-yourself manuals and other forms of record. It is underpinned by many theoretical treatises.

Nevertheless, the central issue of building technologies is often remote, partly tacit. Those in practice have tended not to publish the full richness of their knowledge and experience, their know-how, relying instead on oral traditions and the examples available in existing buildings. Even today, even in highly industrialized economies, this remains largely the case. It may be that the techniques developed in TV for explaining processes will be more appropriate for the analysis of building craft traditions and their mutation into industrial technologies.

I cannot pretend to encompass all this material. This is a preliminary inquiry: to identify why and how certain kinds of knowledge and experience of buildings have been formulated – with particular reference to 'scientific principles' of building.

Building science is concerned to apply the methods and knowledge of general science to the specific issues of buildings. In some areas, this has reached a high level of understanding; in other areas, we are still at the beginning.

Some believe that the scientific study of buildings and people is strictly objective, restricted only by lack of information. This is plainly an oversimplification. Yet the wide array of work under the general heading of building science is of great importance and utility. Immediate questions come to mind: what kind of knowledge is it? How do we make best use of it? First, we need to understand something of its origins and how the ideas emerged.

The question of principles

Are there 'building principles', in the sense of scientific analysis? And in the sense of today's meaning of science? Perhaps they are mostly the principles of natural science, of physics, chemistry and – as we have increasingly come to realize – biology, as applied to buildings, their environments and their implications for the people occupying them.

These principles have had a broader meaning in Western societies, incorporating ideas from mathematics and mensuration (procedures for measurement), the Ancient Greek basis of science. For many in Western countries and elsewhere, 'principles' still includes architectural composition and proportion, established over centuries by a process of (depending upon your standpoint) scientific testing or cultural tradition.

We find these themes in Vitruvius, Roman author from the 1st century BC, whose *Ten Books on Architecture* is the earliest surviving theoretical treatise on building in Western culture and which had renewed impact during the Renaissance. In the initial chapters, he set out the need for scientific understanding of materials, of healthy sites. He formulated the famous dictum of building needing durability, convenience and beauty – the most familiar English translation is 'firmness, commodity and delight'.

The Renaissance also rekindled an awareness of Greek mathematics and theoretical physics which has survived to this day. It combined with the development of experimental science to demonstrate the great power of theory in solving practical problems.

We find, too, an increasing separation of explicit and tacit knowledge as science crystallized out from medieval practices – e.g. astronomy differentiated from astrology, chemistry from alchemy, early medicine from herbalism through the rise of anatomy and pharmacy, and mechanics from practical masonry. There was a further division of labour as those who explored fundamental theories diverged from those who found practical applications.

Since then, the acceleration of science in various cultures has been remarkable. Its effects have continued to permeate the study and practice of building. However, in significant measure, it has to be distinguished from the evolution of building technologies.

The rise of building technologies

Over a similar period, we have seen the rise of various systematic forms of engineering design, although major engineering feats were accomplished earlier, despite the apparent lack of formalized knowledge – e.g. the Pyramids of Ancient Egypt, Roman engineering, the Gothic cathedrals. (The histories of engineering thought are now recognized to be an important field in their own right – partly because we are now more conscious of the fact that many successful technologies preceded the scientific understanding of their behaviour by decades, even centuries.)

With the rise of the world maritime powers – i.e. Portugal, Spain, Holland, France and England – the concept of 'Europe' supplanted that of the Mediterranean as the locus of commercial power in the 16th century. The decline of the Catholic Church was followed by the rise of city states and the absolute monarchies, although Europe continued to be the battleground of warring factions. The emergence of the engineer thus was fuelled by the simultaneous demands of ocean-borne commerce – e.g. for navigation and cartography – and of military confrontation – e.g. fortifications, weapons, machines of war, etc. The term 'civil engineer' emerged to distinguish those practitioners from 'military engineers'. Parallel developments, for instance in 16th century Florence under the Medici family, included the emergence of the architect as a distinct profession.

It was, however, the Industrial Revolution which gave firm definition to the idea of engineering, particularly in building. The distinction between designer and constructor became more marked as the role of the master mason – powerfully established as designer/builder throughout Europe from the 11th century onwards – was supplanted.

The engineer initially was concerned with work with iron-founders, who made engines; they became increasingly involved with building when they helped to design buildings to house the engines and the manufacturing processes thus powered. The iron components they developed were later found to be useful in other buildings and could be used 'off the shelf' by designers.

The structural engineering profession began to emerge during the 18th century as a distinct version of civil engineering. By the 19th century, the advances in mathematical theory and industrial know-how led to a series of spectacular structures, associated with a mastery of metal, glass and masonry. The Crystal Palace in London and the Eiffel Tower in Paris were part of an extraordinary series of demonstration pieces at international exhibitions organized to promote the new industrial powers (did they mark the beginning or the end of an era?). Less obvious but just as significant in their way were a series of metal-framed buildings for commerce and industry.

It was the critical period of the rise of materials and component manufacturing for the building industry; however, it also began a greater fragmentation of technical knowledge which has continued to the present.

This period also saw the transition from the emphasis on invention – based on the independent inventor – to the idea of 'research and development programmes' – based on industrial laboratories. The increased contact which also resulted between industrial development and academic research further contributed to changes in the concepts of science as part of industrial (including military) production.

The rise of building research

With the example of the First World War, and the impact of advanced manufacturing, those concerned with urgent problems in building recognized a need for much more research. The striking successes of scientific (and hence engineering) research, based on fundamental theories of materials, ensured that this became the model for building research from the 1920s onwards. This is enshrined in the character of the Conseil International du Bâtiment (CIB).

The 19th century's legacy of theory in structures, overcoming gravity, and in thermodynamics, understanding energy and its transmission through fluids, was crucial in developing an overall framework of research. This legacy also remains in what is known as the Helmholtz School, from 19th century Vienna (and the intellectual arena of the Austro-Hungarian Empire), which sought to bring medicine more completely into the realm of natural science. Man was treated as any other natural organism, subject to physical science. It was the beginning of psychophysics – the study of sensation, with its mechanistic analyses of sound and hearing, vision, and the other senses. Around the same period, reforms in housing and factory conditions had generated great interest in building comfort, and the combination of practical action and new theories provided a potent mix.

From these two strands eventually grew the exploration of the physiological framework of people's experience of buildings and how this could be expressed as scientific knowledge: explicit, measured, systematically spelled out, based in a general theory, subject to experimental testing – and useful to the designer. This programme continues today, although we have become more conscious of its underlying complexity. Parallel attempts to find similar knowledge through the methods of psychology, sociology and anthropology have been more equivocal.

The empirical knowledge from these endeavours comes in two forms. First, there is that established through statistical and/or experimental procedures. There are several examples. The proof in 19th century London that certain diseases were transmitted in water led to greater control of the water supply, and initiated a surge towards public health engineering more generally (still a vital issue). Systematic tests are used to identify the fire-resistance performance of materials. Other tests are used to define acoustic insulation (i.e. the resistance of a material to the transmission of sound energy through it) and acoustic absorption (i.e. the measure of how much sound energy is reflected from a surface).

Secondly, there is the scientific knowledge derived from investigating well-established procedures but where people did not always know why these methods worked well and therefore could not easily apply them to new situations. (Some authors call this the study of the inherent 'logic' of buildings themselves – e.g. their spatial structure.) The behaviour of masonry domes in large Roman buildings or the structures of Gothic cathedrals provide stark examples: even today, there is still argument about how exactly the antique and medieval masons constructed these extraordinary structures, notwithstanding some famous collapses.

Other examples include the development of reinforced concrete or the evolution of timber-frame construction as it emerged from pragmatic practice into a strong engineering capability based upon calculation.

The evolution of science and technology, within which today's notion of building science is placed, shows us how the very language in which we discuss these matters is also historically bound.

Terminology

To see the changes in language, in terminology, it is instructive to examine historic texts of architecture and building. Gwilt's *An Encyclopedia of Architecture* (London 1867 edition) is a case in point. It is divided into four books, totalling 1364 close-written pages. Book 1 is on the history of architecture; Book 2 is about theory; Book 3 deals with practice; and Book 4 is about money. If we wanted to write such a book today, we might well use the same broad headings.

However, there are some surprises when we see what these terms meant in 1867. 'History' (as might be expected in Victorian England) is dominated by the architecture of Britain, after a perfunctory note on 'wants of Man' ('user requirements' in the language of the 1960s). 'Theory of Architecture' opens with construction, goes on to materials and ends with working drawings – the drawn instructions to site. It contains much of what today we might frame under 'building science' and/or practical building (these two concerns seemed closer then). 'Practice' starts with the classical orders and goes on to proportional systems and typology. The monetary book includes compound interest tables – towards life-cycle costing (costs-in-use) as we would now call it.

The example shows clearly that terms like 'theory' and 'practice' are not neutral, whether related to science or to technology; they shift their meanings over time. They are bound by culture and history. Similar qualifications apply to the concepts of 'scientific principles' and 'technology' themselves.

Further reading

Armytage, W.H.G. (1976), *A Social History of Engineering*, 4th edn, Faber, London.

Banham, R. (1984) *The Architecture of the Well-tempered Environment*, 2nd edn, Architectural Press, London.

Bowley, M. (1960) *Innovations in Building Materials*, Duckworth, London.

Cowan, H.J. (1977) *The Master Builders: A History of Structural and Environmental Engineering from Ancient Egypt to the 19th Century*, Wiley, New York.

Giedion, S. (1950) *Mechanisation Takes Command*, MIT Press, Cambridge, Mass.

Guedes, P. (ed.) (1979) *The Macmillan Encyclopedia of Architecture and Technological Change*, Macmillan, London.

Harvey, D. (1989) *The Condition of Postmodernity*, Basil Blackwell, Oxford.

Herbert, G. (1978) *Pioneers of Prefabrication*, Johns Hopkins University Press, Baltimore, Md.

Kuhn, T.S. (1970) *The Structure of Scientific Revolutions*, 2nd edn, Chicago University Press, Chicago.

Lakatos, I. and Musgrave, A. (eds) (1970) *Criticism and the Growth of Knowledge*, Cambridge University Press, Cambridge.

Laudan, R. (ed.) (1984) *The Nature of Technological Knowledge: Are Models of Scientific Change Relevant?*, D. Reidel, Dordrecht.

Lea, F.M. (1971) *Science and Building: A History of the Building Research Station*, HMSO, London.

Noble, D.F. (1977) *America by Design: Science, Technology, and the Rise of Corporate Capitalism*, Alfred A. Knopf, New York.

Parsons, W.B. (1968) *Engineers and Engineering in the Renaissance* (1939), MIT Press, Cambridge, Mass.

Penrose, R. (1990) *The Emperor's New Mind*, Vintage, London.

Roller, D.H.D. (ed.) (1971) *Perspectives in the History of Science and Technology*, University of Oklahoma Press, Norman, Okla.; see especially C.S. Smith, Art, technology and science: notes on their historical interaction.

CHAPTER TWO

The analysis of sensations

Bums [tramps] are the ideal clients of modern architecture: in perpetual need of shelter and hygiene, real lovers of sun and the great outdoors, indifferent to architectural doctrine and to formal layout.

Rem Koolhaas, 1978

In the study of buildings, we have been particularly concerned with the relation between the weather (a daily result of the prevailing climate) and the comfort of the person in a building.

As we learn more about the energy and material flows which affect bodily comfort, and the ways in which people respond to those flows, we discover that there are more factors which have to be taken into account. They have expanded our concept of the 'comfort zone', the range of given environmental conditions within which we generally feel comfortable. We now speak of the synergy – the combined effect – of different environmental factors: together, their effect may be greater or different than the sum of the individual effects. It marks a change in the relationship between health and comfort as affected by buildings and in the language and concepts we use for their analysis.

This has been notably the case with air quality in buildings, increasingly seen as a key environmental variable. It is a critical flow and, within buildings, air volumes constitute reservoirs for many physical, chemical and biological entities. Indoor air quality – including its physical attributes (temperature, pressure and relative humidity) – is strongly related to outdoor air quality and climate, on which a few remarks are relevant.

Climate

There is an infinite variety of climates around the world. They derive from the interactions of solar radiation and gravitational forces on the atmosphere, together with the differential energy absorption of land, sea and vegetation (e.g. forests). Topographic variations, such as coastal forms, mountain ranges, etc. will further affect the conditions. Nevertheless, there are discernible zones of roughly constant climate, on whose patterns many human activities depend, such as agriculture and vernacular building.

The relationship between climate and health may loom large. In some cases, such as the tropics, the zones may be classified by the atmospheric factors which dominate human comfort in these regions – i.e. air temperature and humidity. These are thus divided:

- **Warm-humid Equatorial** climate (near the Equator: e.g. parts of Tanzania, Singapore, Indonesia).
- **Warm-humid island** climate (e.g. Caribbean islands).
- **Hot-dry desert** climate (e.g. parts of Iraq, Australia).
- **Hot-dry maritime desert** climate (e.g. Kuwait, parts of Pakistan).
- **Composite** or **monsoon** climate (large land masses near the tropics: e.g. parts of India, Burma).
- **Tropical upland** climate (e.g. parts of Mexico, Colombia, Ethiopia, Kenya).

In the case of the UK, by contrast, we find a different kind of description: **temperate-oceanic**. This is because of the confluence of three distinct systems – the warm-wet Atlantic system, dominated by the Gulf Stream, cold from the north and the hot-cold-dry system from continental Europe. The result is a windy country with a regular freeze–thaw cycle. The abrupt UK climate may be good for the skin, but is lethal to many building materials.

Air quality is one of the most critical local environmental factors related to the weather. For instance, many believe that positive ion winds affect people adversely: we know them as the Sirocco, the Foehn, the Mistral, etc. Negative ions (gas molecules with a negative electrical charge) are therefore seen as desirable. Micro-organisms and dusts (such as grass pollen) produce hay fever and other allergic reactions. Atmospheric pressure, as measured on the barometer, can affect moods. The combination of sunlight, ozone and automobile exhaust fumes leads to photochemical smog.

Each climate presents particular problems of achieving human comfort, depending upon the possible built forms and available energy. In addition, the variation of daily weather has to be accommodated as far as possible.

Within such frameworks, designers have to consider the macroclimate of cities and regions and the microclimate of particular buildings. It is a daunting task and, inevitably, there is great reliance on precedent.

Survival and comfort

The 19th-century French physiologist Claude Bernard introduced the idea of the 'internal environment' or 'internal milieu' of the body, the 'soup' of blood and other fluids in which the cells of the body are bathed. It takes the form of distinct volumes called **regulated variables**, which define its constancy. The most important are the gas content of the blood, acidity, sugar content, blood pressure, osmotic pressure and – most significantly for building designers – temperature.

The body's means of achieving stability in these variables is known as **homeostasis**. The internal milieu is itself affected by chemicals, whether produced as part of the homeostatic system (e.g. hormones) or absorbed from the immediate environment (e.g. through the skin or by swallowing, breathing, etc.), whether involuntarily or by deliberate prescription.

In the first – but not final – analysis, comfort can be regarded in terms of the physiological condition and 'biochemical' balance of the body.

Thermal comfort

Thermal comfort is therefore of great interest, because of its crucial role in survival. It represents most clearly the distinction between the conditions we desire and those we are given (the weather).

The deep body temperature of any person must be balanced at

around 37°C, and this balance is maintained between certain limits by the body's homeostatic system.

To cope with a drop in temperature, for instance, the body produces heat through the basal metabolism (i.e. conversion of food) and muscular metabolism (i.e. muscular work, shivering, etc.). It may also gain heat from the environment (e.g. solar radiation, warm air).

Surplus body heat is dissipated by convection (e.g. to immed-iately surrounding air), radiation (e.g. to nearby cold surfaces), conduction (e.g. touching a cold stone wall) or evaporation (e.g. breathing, sweating). Convection and evaporation are affected by air movement (modified by clothing). The rate of evaporation is also affected by the relative humidity of the surrounding air (in turn, related to the barometric pressure). Should these regulatory mechanisms be underdeveloped, as in babies, or break down, as with hyperthermia in old people, the result can be fatal.

Thermal comfort is related to a combination of: the temperature of the surrounding air, relative humidity, radiation and air move-ment. All four factors can be improved or disturbed by the build-ing fabric and building systems, which are intended to keep them within a comfort zone or range to which the body can adjust without stress.

Health and comfort

Makers of buildings hitherto have not seen themselves as respon-sible for the biochemical balance of the human body, although health has often been linked to clean air and water, proper waste disposal and dry shelter (warm or cool, depending on climate).

However, since the 1970s much greater attention has been given to building-related illness (BRI) and sick building syndrome (SBS). This has forced a re-evaluation of substances and organisms to be found in building interiors and of the human responses they induce. (In general, BRI is regarded as sub-chronic illness brought on by a single or just a few factors associated with a building in which the person lives or works, whilst SBS is related to a complex combination of many factors associated with the building.) But problems remain in defining to what extent these conditions (which may cause great distress) are illnesses in the conventional sense. Are these illnesses – at least partially – the result of the same broader social circumstances which have brought these buildings into being?

The discovery of many more factors in the effects of buildings on health has called into question several aspects of modern building design and, by implication, those ways we thought were well established in the past. It has been rather reminiscent of the English author P.G. Wodehouse: he observed the thirteenth chime of the clock – which cast doubt not only upon itself, but also upon the previous twelve . . .

The origins of these factors are various. For instance, we have become acutely aware of how many undesirable elements there are in the external environment which may become concentrated in the reservoirs of the building (e.g. radon).

Surprisingly, perhaps, there are also still some desirable elements in the external environment, but ironically they may be filtered out by the workings of the building (e.g. because of the number of air changes). In some cases, this may be because we have remedied what were seen to be deficiencies in older buildings (e.g. sealing cracks to prevent draughts and heat loss, but thus eliminating accidental ventilation).

The physical materials and components from which the building is constructed may be a source of troublesome materials (e.g. chemical preservative treatments which evaporate into the building's atmosphere, lead piping). This may include the furniture and fittings introduced by the building's occupants (e.g. microfibres and glue solvents from carpet-fitting). It may be, of course, that some such constituents of indoor air are beneficial to the health of the occupants.

The environmental control systems and services are provided precisely to improve comfort and well-being in buildings. It has therefore been something of a shock to their designers to discover the unwanted side-effects of environmental control (e.g. flicker from electric lighting), or the accidental capacities of such systems to harbour harmful organisms (e.g. in wet residues of air conditioning systems).

Manufacturing industry has long been aware of the potential hazards of the equipment installed as part of the building occupants' function. Decades of factory legislation have attempted to keep pace with social concerns about people's conditions of work. Parallel legislation has dealt with conditions in offices. Today we have to recognize that we still have much to learn about the possible health hazards of the new technologies (e.g. radiation from computer screens and ozone from photocopiers).

We introduce many chemical treatments deliberately into the indoor environment (e.g. pesticide sprays and cleaning chemicals). The purpose of these treatments is well-intended, but again we find that – as suggested in Book One – we may unwittingly have created specialized environments in which secondary effects dominate the original intentions.

Finally, we have to acknowledge that the comfort of building occupants may be affected by the social organization of the building (e.g. the degree of control the individual has of their own environment, their own work, etc.).

In unravelling these factors we have to determine which are crucially important, which are within the power of designers and builders to control, and so on. It would be too easy to conclude that it is impossible to build a safe and healthy building.

We must distinguish between different factors:

- Those which are dangerous to health, e.g. disease-carrying organisms ('pathogens' – such as Pontiac Fever), tobacco smoke, asbestos fibres, radon, etc.
- Those which for some people can produce allergic discomfort – 'allergens' (e.g. animal dander, fungal spores).
- Those which can produce some form of psychological discomfort – the term 'psychogens' has been used to characterize the worst effects of social stress at the workplace, noise, flicker from artificial lighting, lack of privacy, job satisfaction – although it is then a complex matter to distinguish these from the psychological consequences of disease.
- Those which have no significant effect on any occupants, so far as is known.
- Those which appear to have beneficial effects on the occupants (e.g. negative ions), to which less attention is currently paid.

Where these disturbances of people's comfort are material – gas/liquid/solid – they often exist at the microscopic scale. Examples include dust and other particles, aerosols (airborne microparticles of liquid) which carry bacteria, microfibres from industrially produced materials, skin flakes and other tokens of the everyday decay of people and animals.

As already noted, various chemicals are introduced into buildings, either as part of the processing of building materials or as surface treatments of materials or as chemical treatments of the interior (e.g. pesticides and cleaning materials). Particular examples are the **volatile organic compounds** (VOC) found in some solvents which are part of adhesives, cleaning materials, surface treatments, etc. In some countries combustion products from cooking or heating may also contaminate the indoor air.

The concept of the internal milieu, introduced above, with its homeostatic responses to disturbances, is directly associated with many of these factors of 'biochemical' comfort.

At one time, if a building's internal environment was considered healthy, it was thought to be comfortable; now we rather assume that if an environment is uncomfortable, it may be unhealthy. Most of the lessons are concerned with what to avoid; we have yet to turn these discoveries to advantage in the active improvement of comfort.

Although we do not yet understand the complex interactions of all these physical, chemical and biological minutiae, a great deal has been learnt about broad design strategies for creating environments in which their effects are diminished. Their discovery has enormously complicated what we now mean by 'comfort zone', but the concept of that zone remains useful.

The sensory basis of comfort

The five senses have critical roles in relation to comfort: sight, hearing, touch, smell and taste. Some are also related to the more general notion of health and comfort, described above.

Visual comfort involves the quality and quantity of lighting, the relation between task lighting and background, the absence of glare, the distribution of colour and texture, the relation between space and light. Only part can be quantified. Today we recognize the need for non-uniform lighting and the balance of 'drama' vs 'efficiency', the need to take account of the complexities to which people respond in the visual environment – i.e. reflectances, colour, texture, changeability, and so on. There is an increasing recognition that our brains/bodies may need daylight for physiological well-being.

Perhaps because of the power of drawing (and drawing conventions) as a means of representing possible buildings, partly because of the dominance of the visual sense in the brain, visual qualities of buildings have been a dominant matter of debate for centuries. It makes plain how important a criterion in perception is the person's *interest*.

Acoustic comfort is one of the most difficult to determine. We have no ear-lids, yet people seem able to tolerate/exclude the most extraordinary noise intrusion whilst listening to or concentrating on something (but sometimes suffering long-term damage to their hearing). It is one of the qualities of buildings which is most perplexing to define: we often refer to the 'feel' of a space or building – and this is partly a matter of its acoustic character. It may also be related to more general vibration – outside the audible range, but none the less perceptible, such as infrasound (lower frequencies than audible) and ultrasound (higher frequencies than audible).

Tactile stimulus and comfort are known to be important to people, especially to babies and small children. This has not been quantified and we rely entirely on the skill of designers and constructors – notably skilled craftsmen – to devise and achieve appropriate treatments in our buildings. Tactile comfort is related also to the body's heat exchange (conduction, radiation) with the materials nearby – the perception of flows between the building and the person.

Smell and taste are important, but have not been the subject of much building research. It may be difficult to relate them to spatial qualities, apart from general ideas of ventilation, although religious institutions have understood their effects for centuries. Perhaps we will explore them further, in the context of our biochemical comfort, with the emerging concerns about the quality of the air that we breathe and the materials it contains. At a simple level, there have been experiments using fragrances in air conditioning (e.g. in Japanese offices), but it is too early to judge how systematically they might be used.

The array of sensory factors has constantly to be related to the space in which the person is placed, the building materials which enclose it and the energy inputs/outputs from the environmental systems. The extent to which these can overcome the variations of external climate and internal function determine how easily the overall condition of the interior is held within the general comfort zone.

The matter can be given a stark recognition if we reflect on the importance of sensory satisfactions for those who cannot easily change their location – e.g. the imprisoned, the disabled, the very young, the old, the infirm. We do not have to design for their circumstances as 'special needs' if we acknowledge the benefits to everybody of good design in these conditions.

Comfort and space

Two other sensory domains are important: **kinaesthetics** – the sense we have of moving through a space; and **proxaemics** – the sense of interpersonal space.

Our experience of moving around buildings is one of the most difficult to describe, let alone to measure, prescribe or predict. Its successful control is one of the special skills of great architects. Because it is a process, rather than a static condition, it cannot easily be represented in drawings. In future, computer animations and other electronic simulations of buildings may help us to penetrate further into this area. At present, we rely greatly on socially established organizations of space – notably the ritual forms of our ceremonial buildings – or on an extraordinary amount of signposting – as in transport terminals.

The distance at which we position ourselves from other people illuminates the idea of space being given meaning by cultural and social context. It is a particular form of comfort, and the comfortable distance varies from nation to nation (or culture to culture) and between social groups (e.g. a person may be uncomfortable if they stand the same distance from a police officer as they would from their spouse, unless they are one and the same). It is affected, amongst other physical factors, by heat exchange (radiation) and smell. The arrangement of buildings may help or inhibit comfortable positioning.

Ergonomics and comfort

The study of **ergonomics**, of the efficient movement of the body in space in relation to defined functional tasks, has made us conscious of the significance of body posture. Studies have been particularly critical to the development of vehicle design, as in automobiles, manned satellites, etc. We also know a certain amount about their significance for furniture design and the design of spaces with highly repetitive functions such as some industrial workplaces, administrative work desks, kitchens, bathrooms, etc.

As more interactive machines enter everyday life, we also notice the ergonomic effects of transfers of work methods devised in different ergonomic contexts – e.g. repetitive strain injuries (RSI), etc. These changes are not invariably problematic, but perhaps more research is needed into ordinary work postures and their implications for building design?

Work in the 1960s by American researcher Alexander Kira demonstrated that bathroom design, including the design of the fittings and the ergonomics of their access, was dominated by cultural factors. Concepts such as cleanliness and privacy are not neutral (indeed, anecdotally, it may be that the concept of privacy exists only in the English language). He showed how variable were the ideas of comfort, odours and personal hygiene.

Task-oriented comfort systems

The American researcher Walter Kroner has identified 'task-oriented comfort systems' (TOCS) as an important aspect of future environmental approaches in buildings, which enable a balanced approach to energy efficiency. The central idea is that we create heterogeneous environments in our buildings, systems in which there is a general background level (e.g. thermal, acoustic, lighting) combined with varying local environments associated with particular tasks, whether work or leisure (e.g. greater air movement, more heat, bright light, etc.). The array of small and portable sources of environmental control (e.g. electric fans, desk lamps, small air conditioners, humidifiers, etc.) shows that we already seek such variety. In hospitals, fire-fighting and various military applications these developments have been taken much further (e.g. in specialized clothing).

The idea of comfort

In building science 'comfort' is principally expressed in terms of human physiology and sensations. But as our responses to external stimuli are informed by sensory perception, they are

affected by experience – personal or social, deliberate or accidental, confusing or coherent, intimate or remote, pleasurable or pain-
ful, mundane or traumatic. Although structured by physiology,
they are also learnt and/or interpreted.

We all know the (primeval?) responses we have to physical
danger or pain, but we know also that particular smells or sights
or sounds are personally evocative. In special cases, we know
that the mind can be trained to overcome inherited or learnt
responses. Can we learn to react calmly to acoustic or thermal
shock? Our perception of the world is bound up with our conception of the world, personal and cultural.

At any one moment, as implied above in the discussion of
'biochemical comfort', a person's state of mind or even their
digestion may temporarily dominate their state of comfort! We
have only to reflect on familiar images of comfort: in a cold
European winter, sitting cosily by the fireside with friends, in a
favourite chair, watching a familiar TV programme; in tropical
humidity, enjoying cool breezes after a satisfying meal, reading a
favourite book. We have some holistic concept of total comfort,
only part of which is determined by the building and services: the
book may be as important as the room.

Some researchers have also been concerned about the level of
complexity in the environmental conditions we seek: too little
will appear bland or boring, too much will be confusing and
disorienting. This may be linked to the notion of task-oriented
comfort systems.

In such circumstances, the idea of comfort cannot be universal or
objective, although we may be able to generalize sufficiently to devise useful guidelines and international standards. This is why it is
possible to raise the standard of comfort, so that a level which was
acceptable a few centuries ago may now be perceived as deprivation. For instance, in many Western countries, we now expect to be
able to wear summer clothing all the year round in our buildings.

We have also to remember that technical standards are culture-
bound: a study in the 1960s revealed that minimum standards
of illumination for common buildings (e.g. hospital operating
theatres) varied between industrialized countries by 1:5. All too
often, the critical pursuit of technical understanding is justified
as being 'objective', when this is neither necessary nor well-
founded. The point is made in graffiti discovered at Princeton
University and reported in *New Scientist* magazine:

$$2 + 2 = 5 \quad \text{(for sufficiently large values of 2).}$$

Beyond this relativity, the dilemma of seeking an ever greater degree of commonality, with its benefits of shared knowledge, is that we may suppress those local cultural meanings which are important to people.

We may need to define different objectives at different scales of the built environment, recognizing that new technologies will allow us to provide to the individual a much greater personal control of their local environment. This acknowledges not only psychological concerns, and the fact that people's reactions to a given environmental level will vary in a personal way, perhaps in terms of what some call 'bio-rhythms', but that the local conditions vary extraordinarily.

Although we can control some aspects of behaviour through buildings (e.g. mostly with doors or stairs – ask the physically disabled), it is unclear how far we can (or even want to) control perception. The concept of comfort and the dimensions of perception provide a constant set of dilemmas of design.

Some researchers have even begun to question whether the concept 'comfort' is really that useful as a guide for designers and builders, when we might rather search for a broader concept of sensory experience in buildings, even united with wider social and cultural considerations. The greater understanding of comfort and health, or whatever concepts come to replace them in buildings, and eventually more systematically on building sites and in other areas of production, serves only to underline the complexity of the task and the need for robust strategies in the solutions.

Further reading

Attali, J. (1985) *Noise: The Political Economy of Music* (1977) (trans. B. Massumi), Theory and History of Literature, Vol. 16, Manchester University Press, Manchester.

Curwell, S., March C. and Venables, R. (eds) (1990) *Buildings and Health*, RIBA Publications, London.

Fanger, P.O. (1970) *Thermal Comfort*, McGraw-Hill, New York.

Goffman, E. (1963) *Behavior in Public Places*, Free Press, Glencoe, Ill.

Hall, E.T. (1959) *The Silent Language*, Doubleday, Garden City, NY.

Hall, E.T. (1966) *The Hidden Dimension*, Doubleday, Garden City, NY.

Koenigsberger, O.H., Ingersoll, T.G., Mayhew, A. and Szokolay, S.V. (1974)

Manual of Tropical Housing and Building. Pt 1, Climatic Design, Longman, London.

Kira, A. (1967) *The Bathroom*, Bantam Books, New York.

Kroner, W.M. (ed.) (1988) *A New Frontier: Environments for Innovation*, Proceedings of International Symposium on Advanced Comfort Systems for the Work-environment, Center for Architectural Research, Rensselaer Polytechnic Institute, Troy, New York, May; see especially J.W. and D.R. Heerwagen, Holes in the fabric of 'comfort': what one's state of mind has to do with one's bodily state.

Mach, E. (1959) *The Analysis of Sensations*, 5th edn (1906) (trans. S. Waterlow), Dover, New York.

Rapoport, A. and Watson, N. (1967–8) Cultural variability in physical standards. *Transactions of the Bartlett Society*, **6**.

Vincent, J.D. (1990) *The Biology of Emotions* (trans. J. Hughes), Basil Blackwell, Oxford.

CHAPTER THREE

The analysis of energy

Buildings are prey to various forms of energy – electromagnetic (e.g. solar radiation) and kinetic (e.g. noise). These forms may be deliberate, unavoidable, externally supplied or internally generated. They may be essential (e.g. electric power), insignificant (e.g. moonlight) or catastrophic (e.g. earthquakes). We have to make provision for those that noticeably affect the function or durability of buildings.

Energy and environment

The sun and the moon provide much of the available power for providing and running our buildings, one way or another, and this emphasizes the inextricable link between global energy and the broad environment in understanding energy efficiencies.

Whether renewable or non-renewable, most energy sources provide us with dilemmas, only some of which are resolved by market forces. The UK economist Barbara Ward noted that the industrialized countries had enjoyed a '25-year cheap energy jag' until 1973, developing oil-dependent industries and transport. The rapid improvement in thermal comfort standards in buildings of these countries, with consequent expectations in other poorer countries, was but one effect which it is now difficult to reverse.

In the past twenty years or so, however, we have also become sharply conscious of the environment debit associated with the production of certain forms of fuel and energy – e.g. the effluent from power stations, the risk of oil spillage from supertankers, desertification from collecting firewood, ecological change brought about by hydroelectric schemes, etc. The issue is associated with low and high technologies alike and some have argued accordingly that the solution is to maximize the use of human labour in building production and the activities contained in buildings. This presents severe problems when applied to large conurbations, especially with the pace of urbanization and increasing employment in manufacturing and indoor service activities.

The sun's electromagnetic energy (radiation) is absorbed through photosynthesis into plants, which over millennia are converted into non-renewable fossil fuels: peat, coal, natural gas and oil.

There is discussion as to whether nuclear power is renewable or not, but despite its short-term attraction of not emitting atmospheric pollutants, waste disposal and the catastrophic effects of a major accident make its environmental assessment problematic.

Alternative sources of energy

The array of renewable energy sources – some of which dominated our use before the Industrial Revolution – include:

- **bio-fuels** – organic materials (timber, increasingly a cash crop for many uses; crops for liquid fuels; digestion of sewage and wet waste; incineration of refuse and crop wastes; landfill gases);
- **wind**;
- **water** (tidal barrages; wave power; hydroelectric power from rivers/dams; heat pumps into rivers);
- **geothermal reservoirs** (hot dry rock; aquifers);
- **solar energy** (active heating/cooling; passive heating/cooling; photo-voltaic).

It seems very likely in future that electricity and solar energy will be even more the predominant modes by which end-use energy is supplied to many buildings, at least in the industrialized countries, and probably for most large cities. In some countries, district heating schemes and combined heat/power schemes will also play significant roles.

Energy absorbed in buildings

When we ask how much of our energy consumption is concerned with buildings, we have to examine the complete processes of manufacture, assembly and use. This is more complex than might appear at first thought. We can identify the following elements of energy consumption:

- Manufacture of machines used in the building processes,
- Extraction of materials,
- Transport of materials,
- Conversion and manufacture of materials and components,
- Transport of materials and components to merchants or to site,
- Assembly on site,
- Occupancy (space heating; water heating; air tempering and ventilation; lighting; power supply to machines),
- Maintenance and cleaning,
- Refurbishment or further building works,
- Demolition,
- Recycling of materials and disposal.

This complexity raises the question as to whether we can ever adequately calculate the real energy and environmental cost of a method of building. For instance, materials which are good thermal insulants – such as timber, certain plastic foams, etc. – and thus enable efficiencies which reduce the cost of space heating of buildings, may have severe penalties elsewhere in the multiple equation. Too great a use of timber may have unwanted effects on rain forests. The gases used in foaming some plastics may attack the ozone layer of the upper atmosphere.

In the absence of clear-cut evidence, four guidelines may be helpful when considering energy in buildings. Two are concerned with the building's relation to the sun. First, the designer can affect the solar energy equation by choice of orientation – the effect of physical shape on flow. Secondly, external controls – such as blinds, adjustable if possible, will enable the best control of the flow of radiant energy. This is a more abstract effect of 'shape' on energy flows. Thirdly, the thermal capacity of the building – its ability to act as a heat reservoir – has to be carefully examined in the specific environment and context. Finally, energy consumption can be affected by efficiency of the fabric –

good thermal insulation and low heat loss generally, increasing the 'reservoir capacity' – although we have also to bear in mind the problems of ventilation, condensation and the need in certain buildings to dispose of wild heat output from machines.

We can also extend these ideas to the consideration of the external microclimate of buildings, and their mediation of the internal climates.

In the absence of better judgement, reducing the energy demands of building use and improving the building's effectiveness as a controllable reservoir remain important strategies for utilizing the energies which flow into buildings.

The dilemma remains: can we ever know enough to obtain a suitable balance between the conflicting demands (and conflicting they often are) of energy efficiency, minimizing energy consumption, environmental sensitivity, human health and comfort, and appropriate technologies in areas of increasing population density?

Further reading

Fathy, H. (1986) *Natural Energy and Vernacular Architecture*, University of Chicago Press, Chicago.

Markus, T.A. and Morris, E.N. (1980) *Buildings, Climate and Energy*, Pitman, London.

This Common Inheritance: Britain's Environmental Strategy, Cm 1200, HMSO, London, September 1990.

CHAPTER FOUR

Building engineering

Building design is confronted with the resolution of time, cost and performance in the pursuit of quality. Today this underpins what are known as **value engineering** – an approach by which supposed sub-systems in a design are further optimized against a constant performance requirement – and **quality assurance** – production management frameworks in which the potentials for error and sub-optimization are anticipated and reduced. Like some illnesses: early on the diagnosis is difficult but the treatment has a better chance of success; later on, diagnosis is more secure but the treatment is difficult.

This chapter explores a few of the alternative descriptions of buildings we know as **sub-systems**, those to which a substantial amount of engineering expertise has been devoted.

Structural behaviour

Structural design in buildings is rarely at the limit of our theoretical knowledge, by contrast with large-scale civil engineering. The recent advent of computer programs of great sophistication, such as in finite element analysis, has meant even greater ability to deal with difficult structures – including those for which our theoretical methods are at the limit. However, it remains an enormously complex matter, by virtue of the nature of the building process and the demands of building form.

The crucial parameters of a building structure are: shape or geometry; support or structural action (including geotechnics);

processes of manufacture and assembly; the material(s) from which it is made; its connections – between discrete parts of the structure and between the structure and other elements of the building. Much research has been done to further our understanding in all of these parameters, with the possible exception of shape – the attribute whose practical understanding is longest established.

Shape is concerned with the relation between the structure as a distinct entity and the building as a whole, with the definition of interior spaces. It is also concerned with types of structural action, basic stiffness and efficient resistance to deformations (such as buckling). Moreover, it is the shape of the structure (including structural contributions from various parts of the building not formally treated as 'structure') which defines the flow of forces/energies, their concentration in reservoirs at discontinuities (such as cracks), and so on.

A good example in the extreme is the repertory of structural shapes which intrinsically are more resistant to earthquake forces. Those to be preferred have regular forms and low centres of gravity: the compositional tendencies of classical architecture towards bi-axial symmetry in plan, high central blocks and cellular spaces also happen to be advantageous in earthquake zones.

The qualitative understanding of shape within the whole building is the root of good structure.

Structural action deals with supposed behaviour, for which we invoke methods of analysis, on the assumption of a distribution of forces induced by gravity, wind, etc. The specific action is, of course, affected by shape, which is more easily analyzed quantitatively if the shape derives from some regular geometry which can be described mathematically. It is the 'interior story' of the structure which may, of course, behave differently from our theoretical assumptions.

If the structure is highly responsive to predicted loads – e.g. as in lightweight membrane structures – and deflects considerably, this has important implications for the detailing of both the structure and the attached enclosure: conventional construction does not usually have to cope with large movements of this kind.

Processes of manufacture and assembly may loom large in structural design. A structure may be optimized in terms of efficient use of material but may be sub-optimal in terms of the building as a whole: it may be awkward to make or it may present diseconomies in other elements. Conversely, it may be sensible to sub-optimize the structural design to simplify on-site assembly or the connections of other components.

An example of shape and production coming together can be found in the hyperbolic paraboloid shells of reinforced concrete built in Mexico during the 1960s (Fig. 4). The shape is mathematically describable and inherently stiff. The framework, however, is made from straight pieces of timber, which can be re-used. The shell is very thin, as there is little bending – this is all transferred to the edges and supports. As a result, it is well suited to a building industry where labour is cheap and materials are expensive.

Figure 4 Reinforced concrete hyperbolic paraboloid shell structure. This is a very efficient use of the steel reinforcement and concrete as structure. The curves are generated from straight lines, so that the temporary formwork needed to create the 'mould' for the shell can be made from straight pieces of timber – cheap and re-useable.

Choices of material are, of course, closely related to the previous three parameters. Certain shapes maximize the benefit of specific material properties. Some materials may present non-structural problems such as the behaviour of steel structures in fire.

Processes of manufacture or assembly are crucial issues in building structures, as the whole structure is often on the critical path of the building programme. The need for temporary works may be affected by shape and material. With prefabricated elements, the loads experienced during transport and erection (Figs 5 and 6) may be more critical than any experienced once in service.

Finally, the nature of connections within a structure may significantly affect site assembly, as well as the appearance of the final building. Connections between the structure and other elements are affected by the structural material and shape and also have important ramifications for the assembly processes. Connections of both kinds ensure that building structures are very complex at a secondary level, by virtue of uncalculable

Figure 5 Moving house. This activity places unusual loads on the structure. Photo © Sally and Richard Greenhill.

Figure 6   Moving house.

stiffness from non-structural members such as window frames, and often may be described as 'semi-determinate' with factors of safety rather different from those which have been calculated.

It is clear that, in practice, the making of a building structure is only partly dominated by the problem of analysis and calculation.

Fire engineering

A fire involves the explosive transfer of matter into energy through an irreversible chemical change. It suddenly changes the flows of energy (kinetic and electromagnetic) around the space of its origin, using radiation and the internal air as the immediate conduits, but – if unchecked – it will transfer sufficient energy into solid materials and either ignite them (if they evolve flammable gases) or those to which they, in turn, transfer energy.

To fight the fire, we introduce flows of liquid and gases – water, carbon dioxide, etc. These either change the accelerating chemical reactions of combustion and/or transfer and dissipate the thermal energy. To save any people concerned, we provide protected channels for their safe escape.

Fire regulations for buildings are notoriously fraught. Designers often appear to find them awkward to apply, particularly if this is not done until late in the design process. Constructors may well discover that some structural fire precautions are difficult to install on site, especially with complex service connections coming through supposedly compartmented spaces. But today we have become aware that a critical factor is human behaviour during building occupation.

Fire risks include:

- **life safety** (e.g. exposure to toxic gases, hot air, panic, rate of fire growth);
- **conflagration** (e.g. fire load, rate of fire growth, spread of hot gases);
- **protection of property** (e.g. chance of ignition, structural damage, consequential losses).

Fire safety strategies may be considered under three headings:

- **structural fire precautions** (including the various passive measures);
- **means of escape** (including personnel training and management);
- **fire-fighting equipment, installations** (including active systems such as sprinklers, reversible-thrust fans, automatic shutters) and **access**.

All of these are affected by human behaviour at a moment when the building may not be in the condition assumed for the purposes of estimating fire safety.

To resolve structural fire precautions we have to distinguish combustible and non-combustible materials, that is, those with undesirable properties of energy absorption. For combustible materials, there are classifications of 'surface spread of flame' to help determine whether they may be used in specified conditions. These properties, in effect, define the capacity of reservoirs of material in relation to the absorption of thermal energy from combustion.

The principal and traditional means of achieving fire safety for the occupants is through the use of fire compartments – walls and floors with defined fire resistance (boundary conditions to the 'reservoir'). A fire is then contained whilst occupants escape.

Fire control is concerned with the preservation of distinct

reservoirs and the maintenance of boundaries. There has been increased interest in recent years in so-called 'active' fire precautions, methods which rely on electrical/mechanical services to help control the fire. In effect, this approach attempts to change the conditions of the initial reservoirs of air and combustible material, to partition a given volume of air into smaller volumes which are more easily controlled, before the fire gathers momentum. It is also worthy of note that flame and combustion gases in a burning building exhibit all the characteristics of chaotic systems.

Environmental controls

The short traditional realm of the mechanical and electrical services engineers has broadened in the second half of the 20th century to an extraordinary degree. Yet the extent to which they can control environmental comfort is limited.

Thermal comfort depends on four factors (air temperature, radiation, air movement and relative humidity), whose perception is affected by a person's clothing. The mechanical engineer can expect to control only one of these (air temperature) with any degree of certainty, subject to the heat transmittance of the building fabric (defined by the architect/designer). If the building is air-conditioned, then relative humidity can also be closely controlled.

Air movement is highly dependent upon how the users organize themselves and the building, although the architect/designer can make a major contribution through the organization of volumes and layers of air throughout the building, and their connection to the outside.

Radiation exchange of the human body with adjacent surfaces is within the control of the architect/designer, through specification of materials and finishes, but again this will be affected by actions of the users (e.g. clothing, adding pin-up boards).

It follows that a significant amount of strategic decisions for thermal comfort are within the overall building design. This underlines the importance of not asking the specialist engineer to 'make things work' only when the built form and material choices have been largely determined. A similar argument arises for visual and acoustic design.

Lighting design

Perhaps the most critical desired quality of natural light in buildings is that it remain 'natural'. That is, we seek to maintain its qualities of intensity, colour rendering, directionality, and change with the weather and time of day. We may well prefer these qualities to penetrate even deep-plan buildings, whilst controlling energy efficiency.

Where we seek to differ from the outdoors is in the highlighting of the building fabric – the use of wash and accents on surfaces, the use of light from multiple sources, the special focus on tasks requiring carefully controlled local light.

The Finnish architect Alvar Aalto, a virtuoso of the imaginative control of both natural and artificial lighting, has shown how the design of the fundamental built form and the configuration of openings can achieve these ends. In his case, light is brought into the building to define the functional character of the spaces, including the comfort of the occupants. In his designs, windows exist principally to admit light, rather than to offer views; the opposite argument is often promoted today, as we come to rely more on artificial systems for illumination.

Although today we have the most remarkable array of artificial lighting systems, the use of multiple switching, computer controls and dimmers has removed the need for tight design of lighting provision. We have moved to a more theatrical concept of lighting, in which people can create a more personal lighting context.

Acoustic design

Acoustic design is at its limits in large concert halls. Without amplification, we seek the acoustic equivalent of both the telescope and the microscope. The principal manner in which this is achieved is to retain as much as possible of the initial sound energy, to preserve its character. We should minimize absorption within the space. A building is not a musical instrument, since we retain rather than distribute the sound.

Recent research on concert halls has shown the importance of cross-reflections to our perception of the quality, richness and intelligibility of music. (We seek slightly different qualities in listening to speech.) Optical geometry inscribed on building sections is very misleading and modern computer methods for depicting the three-dimensional character of sound dispersal are more reliable.

The other broad principle of good acoustic design rests in the building plan. It is to ensure that the various spaces are suitable acoustic neighbours, to avoid an over-reliance on the sound insulation of the building fabric. It is a strategy for the disposition of reservoirs around the building, to control the relationships between flows of sound energy and the location of acoustically sensitive activities.

Finally, it may be apparent that many of these environmental factors are dominated not only by the form of the building, but by the size of the spaces concerned. The volume of air per person – and its arrangement in a system of reservoirs – may be the single most critical environmental variable for comfort in many buildings.

Cost analyses

A crucial inheritance from the methods of the 19th century in analysing buildings was the tendency to reduce things to their constituent elements. This has been particularly powerful in the evolution of cost analyses – i.e. the development of a design strategy and solution techniques for the financial arrangements of a building project.

The financial evaluation of a building project may include the following:

- land costs;
- infrastructure costs;
- initial building costs;
- disruption costs (e.g. decanting employees during construction work);
- fitting-out costs (including the expensive machines now installed in many buildings);
- refitting or rehabilitation costs;
- running and maintenance costs;
- potential rent or sale value or other income from the building;
- potential asset value;

- opportunity costs (i.e. of alternative projects which could have been financed from the same resources);
- the cost of employing the people to work in the building over its useful life.

In many instances, land costs and the costs of employing people to work in the building may dominate the equation. For this reason, good design and construction are important because they will make those people's occupation of the building more efficient, comfortable and pleasurable. They may also enhance the rent or asset value. Since the cost of design services is a small proportion of the initial building cost, which in turn may be a small proportion of the total project investment, the value-for-money return on good design is substantial. A similar argument applies to the contribution of skilled builders. For there is no reason to believe that using able designers and builders costs much more in fees than to use incompetents.

The discussion of initial building cost may be pursued further. One division of a building is into five technical elements, as in the work of American architect Gregory Turner:

- **podium** (e.g. ground works, vertical transport);
- **structure** (including integral finishes);
- **envelope** (where it is non-structural);
- **machinery** (e.g. environmental, fire safety, security);
- **infill** (internal divisions which are non-structural and non-mechanical, including finishes).

Turner has established evidence that for centuries in Western culture the initial cost of non-residential buildings was dominated by that of the structure – something like 70% of total first cost in the case of King's College Chapel, Cambridge (1446), or the Uffizi Gallery in Florence (1560). Of course, at that time much of the building envelope was integral with the structure. However, this proportion did not change very greatly until the advent of metal frame structures in the 19th century, since when the proportion has dropped to under 20%. Spatial benefits have also followed with the reduction of plan area devoted to structure.

By contrast, it is only in the 20th century that infill costs have exceeded about 10% of first cost. The podium cost remained fairly constant, between 7% and 12%. The envelope cost grew from medieval times, when it was around 10%, towards 20% this century.

The extraordinary change, which of course has affected the proportion attributable to structure, is in the provision of machinery. This has risen from a negligible figure in the medieval period, still under 10% in the 19th century, to around 30% in the first half of the 20th century. Since then, its dominance has increased further, especially in buildings with special servicing requirements (e.g. modern finance houses, some factories, etc).

Similar broad trends are evident in houses, according to Turner, although the structure did not have quite the same early dominance. Infill and envelope costs today are quite significant, having grown steadily from medieval days on.

The use of elemental cost analyses, based on historical data, presents many problems when new designs and/or new production methods are introduced. In particular, it is insensitive to the complexity of construction method. It is nevertheless a revealing method for understanding the economic significance of industrial change.

The other crucial concern of cost engineering is the process of establishing the price for the building contract. There is an extraordinary variety of methods for procuring buildings and hence of how the price is determined.

The assumption is that, as with the elemental cost analyses, the costs of building work are known historically and that the cost of a proposed building can be built up from this base. The price follows.

The UK mathematician Brian Fine has, however, questioned whether this process is as objectively based as is claimed. He explores – as others have done – the critical difference between price and cost, suggesting that much less is known about true costs than may be claimed. He has argued that the price emerges from a process dominated by social factors (part of which he describes as witchcraft!), by the culture of the building industry on a very local basis. The price then becomes the controlling variable on the building process, a target to which the organization aims rather than a true description of real costs: if it appears that costs will excessively undershoot or overshoot the target, avoiding action is taken.

If we seek comparisons of construction costs between different countries, we find a balance (defined by UK quantity surveyor

James Meikle) between 'comparability' and 'representativeness'. That is, the more a building is typical of its country's building industry, the less it may be comparable to one of the same notional type in another country, and vice versa.

Once again, in these two examples we discover dynamic processes, informed by feedback systems, with the controlling variables established on a rational, culturally determined basis.

Further reading

Arnold, C. and Reitherman, R. (1982) *Building, Configuration and Seismic Design*, Wiley, New York.

Brandon, P.S. (ed.) (1982) *Building Cost Techniques: New Directions*, Spon, London.

Coe, P. and Reading, M. (1981) *Lubetkin and Tecton*, Arts Council of Great Britain, Bristol.

Faber, C. (1963) *Candela: The Shell Builder*, Architectural Press, London.

Forsyth, M. (1985) *Buildings for Music*, Cambridge University Press, Cambridge.

Harlow, P. (ed.) (1980–5) *The Practice of Site Management* (3 vols), Chartered Institute of Building, Englemere, Ascot.

Hillier, B., Musgrove, J. and O'Sullivan, P. (1972) Knowledge and design. *Proceedings of the EDRA Conference*, EDRA, Los Angeles, Calif.

Meikle, J.L. (1990) International comparisons of construction costs and prices. *Habitat International*, **14**, 2–3, 185–92.

Olgyay, A. and Olgyay, V. (1957) *Solar Control and Shading Devices*, Princeton University Press, Princeton, NJ.

Orton, A. (1988) *The Way We Build Now*, Van Nostrand Reinhold, Wokingham.

Architecture + Urbanism, March 1989; Special issue on Renzo Piano: Building Workshop, 1964–88.

Salvadori, M. and Heller, R. (1975) *Structure in Architecture*, 2nd edn, Prentice-Hall, Englewood Cliffs, NJ.

Topliss, C. (1982) *Demolition*, Longman, London.

Turin, D.A. (ed.) (1975) *Aspects of the Economics of Construction*, George Godwin, London.

Gregory Turner, R. (1986) *Construction Economics and Building Design: A Historical Approach*, Van Nostrand Reinhold, New York.

CHAPTER FIVE

Building pathology and its lessons

It is somewhat meaningless to speak of a building's lifetime. Foundations may survive for a thousand years, whilst the roof structure may be replaced after a thousand months. The sanitary fittings in the bathroom could last a thousand weeks, the external paintwork a thousand days, and the light bulbs a thousand hours. How old is the building? If we recognize the role of continuous piecemeal maintenance, the calculation becomes even more tortuous. It is, however, very worthwhile to discuss the significance of time in building affairs.

Time in building affairs

Building pathology is the study of failures over time in building materials and components. In particular, it deals with situations where durability does not fulfil expectations.

Buildings degrade over time, owing to a variety of environmental flows, including:

- Air (e.g. wind forces, chemical contaminants, oxidation);
- Water (e.g. from the air, ground; chemical contaminants; condensation; materials drying out);
- Solar radiation (e.g. temperature, ultraviolet);
- Mechanical damage;
- Matter (physical, chemical, biological).

The mechanism of change also may be physical, chemical, biological or some combination. The speed at which this occurs depends on the micro-environment, the location and the work-manship of the construction.

If a material is inherently incapable of withstanding predict-able flows and degradation within a reasonable period, it must be protected by barriers, covers, additives, surface treatments, detailing, maintenance or frequent replacement (as in rural build-ing in poor countries).

In certain climates and contexts, failure patterns can be domi-nated by particular flows. For instance, in the UK it is plain that water is a prevailing problem area, as the freeze–thaw cycle predominates. This is because water is the only material which flows in all phases (vapour, liquid and ice) and therefore can move between different kinds of reservoir. It also has a particular relationship with organic materials and biological agents.

There are three principal categories of material which dominate our studies of durability:

1. Non-metallic minerals (e.g. brick, stone, glass).
2. Metallic minerals (e.g. iron, aluminium).
3. Organic polymers (e.g. timber, plastics, paints).

Non-metallic minerals are generally very durable. They are strong in compression and unpredictable in tension. Failure tends to occur in a brittle manner, in some instances because of the material's porosity, in various forms. The most obvious is water penetration (followed by frost cycles or the precipitation of soluble salts). There are several forms of biological attack (e.g. fungal growth), chemical attack (e.g. acid rain, sulphate attack) or physical attack (e.g. mechanical damage). We have also to remember the problems of excessive loading (especially dynamic or cyclic loading) and temperature movement.

Metals tend to revert to their 'natural' state in the presence of oxygen and moisture, notably when the relative humidity ex-ceeds 70%. This corrosion is an electrolytic process leading to oxidation. Some oxides (e.g. rusting of iron) are disintegrative; others (e.g. aluminium) protect the metal beneath. The process may be accelerated by atmospheric pollution, adjacent materials which are chemically active (e.g. steel touching aluminium), stress and temperature.

Organic polymers vary in their resistance to water-based attack, their principal problem. Some (e.g. paints, mastics) are specifically water-resisting materials, although they may be damaged by water penetration behind them leading to mechanical failure. Others – particularly timber – are highly susceptible when the moisture content exceeds 20% or when it changes significantly. Insect and fungal attack are repelled by poisoning the cell materials which provide food to these parasites.

Linked to this water-based attack is the question of temperature movement of polymeric materials. This may lead to distortion and/or degradation. Ultraviolet radiation affects all polymers, through its attack on the molecular structure.

Synergistic failures

Some of the most perplexing failures occur through very complex combinations of factors, partly inherent in material properties, partly arising through the configurations of construction and microenvironment. Some arise because of the use of impervious materials on the assumption that they can be constructed without damage. Many involve some form of condensation in unexpected volumes of the building.

At the core of this analysis is the simple fact that we try to make the interior conditions of the building different from those outside. This creates a potential or gradient, as discussed in Book One, and induces various flows of energy, air, vapour, small particles, etc. The more we have sought to increase the differences (e.g. by ensuring less variation internally than externally), the more we will tend to induce such flows. Ironically, the attempt to exercise greater control has led to larger differentials which, in turn, require still greater control.

Movement arises as reservoirs change content with flows of energy or matter; boundaries may be eroded or scoured through the changes mentioned above. Patterns of this kind may be modelled through the new techniques of diffusion limited aggregation (DLA), which allow mathematical modelling and computerized display of many natural growth patterns (e.g. lightning paths, cracks in brittle materials, etc.).

One failure pattern recently identified by the London architectural firm of Bickerdike Allen Partners is of great theoretical and practical interest: it is called **thermal pumping**. Sealed insulation voids close to the outer face of the building envelope will heat and cool. The internal pressure changes accordingly. This creates a pumping potential towards the interior and/or exterior. Air drawn in may be warm and humid, condensing some of its vapour as liquid water on contact with the cooler surfaces of the void. As pressures reverse with changes in external conditions, the liquid is then pumped out – sometimes down through ceilings, giving the appearance of failure in the external envelope. The volumes in which this can occur are also often prime candidates for corrosion or fungal attack.

It will be apparent that this is an excellent example of the argument set out in this text. Problems arose because of the unwitting creation of discrete reservoirs in the building fabric, and their positioning, such that a potential was set up between them. Why do these reservoirs occur? Do they occur more frequently in modern construction than in earlier decades?

One issue is that of improved engineering of the building fabric. This has meant the successful attempt to use less material more efficiently in achieving stiff structures. Almost inevitably, one of the by-products has been more entrapped air voids or more space between the pieces of material. Where these voids are supposedly well sealed, they are then vulnerable to errors in assembly on site such as water gathered whilst not properly covered, or vapour control layers being perforated. They are also vulnerable when other mechanisms come into play such as hairline cracks from movement or shrinkage (from wet materials drying out). These breaks may only become a route for unintended flows when the pressure or potential is sufficiently strong, creating 'point loads' far in excess of those for which the system has been designed.

A further flow-based failure pattern is stress corrosion of metals, where the synergy of energy and matter has led to an overloading of the capacity of the metal.

In general terms, then, filters can become reservoirs (e.g. filters in air-conditioning systems); reservoirs can become channels for unexpected transfers.

Deliberate reservoirs

It is interesting to note that one trend in modern construction has been to introduce intermediate environments and voids in construction, intermediate reservoirs in the possible flow routes.

The first example is the renamed **atrium** building, in which a large volume of air is contained within the building to act as an intermediate stage between the main volumes for people and the outside. This has built on energy studies and other analyses following the development of 19th century buildings with large areas of glass enclosure. The controlled energy from the sun and the use of air as an insulant are the critical flow conditions.

The second development is the repositioning of thermal insulation outside the main building fabric. This involves the so-called inverted roof system for flat roofs and rainscreen cladding for the vertical enclosure (one version of which involves balancing pressures between the exterior and the enclosed volumes). Both introduce reservoirs of air into zones where they can be systematically linked to the outside air, at a suitable temperature, thus preventing the creation of condensation zones.

This layering of the building volume is reminiscent of the system of successively hotter chambers in Turkish baths, where the temperature difference between adjacent chambers is not great, but that between the innermost and the outermost is substantial.

Simultaneously, of course, we also find a contrary trend, namely the combination of the entire external enclosure into one composite cladding element, which provides exterior finish, full range of performance attributes, and the interior finish: it has only to be bolted into position.

In the one case, the range of performance attributes are, in a sense, separated out and each attribute is given its physical element. In the other case, they are all combined, so that one physical element may serve several performance requirements. It is another example of the bipolar nature of building: some seek the single integrated model; others the disaggregated elemental model.

Building failures

It is plain that we shall have to develop various definitions of building failure. One version emerges from the combination of studying flows of matter and energy, evolution of technologies and concepts of robust technology. The general epidemics of building failures, especially amongst apparently well-established methods of building, should also be understood as an indicator of industrial change.

Beyond this, we can envisage the description of technical systems in terms of their 'core' functions and their 'key' functions, where core functions are the principal purposes and key functions are subsidiary systems (e.g. fire protection to structural steelwork), necessary so that the core functions can be sustained. In turn, we can see that in many cases any one core or key function both supports and is supported by other core and key functions in other elements. It is thus a complex matter to clarify on what performance stability a given system depends; and, as a corollary, failure of the system may be a result of failure of either a core or a key function, or even of a function in some other element upon which that performance indirectly depends.

Measuring behaviour

The difficulty with building pathology is that, as with all pathology, it assumes a normality and a predictability. Building failures appear to be deterministic but unpredictable, chaotic, significantly affected by small differences in the initial conditions. A flow-based analysis appears therefore to be a useful addition to its analytical armoury.

The time-based analysis of buildings we have used to date can be compared to the showing of a movie of an athlete running the 100m. We can show the movie in real time and observe the pattern of the race. We can show it slowed down, and discover that whatever speed the athlete is at, he or she always hits the ground with the foot exactly below the centre of gravity. We can show it speeded up and obtain a stroboscopic effect, where the smoothness or jerkiness of the athlete's movements is most visible. At whatever speed we examine the moving image, regularities appear. But the movie is constructed of stills: slow it down enough and this is apparent. The task is to find a way of recording the dynamic qualities of genuine flow.

In the analysis of building behaviour, we have begun to develop a large repertoire of non-destructive testing methods. Many have started as methods for investigating the behaviour of individual elements, materials or components such as ultrasonics and X-rays in checking welds. They are often laboratory based. However, the more recent trend has begun to confront the problem of assessing whole-building behaviour. Examples include: the use of radar for investigating geotechnical behaviour of the ground; wind tunnels to judge wind patterns around buildings; thermography to identify leakages of thermal energy; large machines, not unlike vacuum cleaners, which can measure air infiltration rates; computer-based modelling of internal air flows (through computational fluid dynamics (CFD) methods) to describe fire behaviour, location of contaminated air, etc; many other techniques which have started life in the world of remote sensing. Many of these techniques have been driven initially by the desire to understand the energy consumption of buildings.

It is interesting to speculate whether we might convert some of these measuring methods into whole building assessment methods, to take account of (for example) green issues, construction quality (the amount of air leakage could be an indicator of construction quality?), etc. To do so, we invoke the ideas of flows and shape discussed in Book One.

We can generalize from what has already been done: by directing flows of specific energy and/or matter at buildings, we may discover useful information from the measurement of their responses, and the location of nodes which absorb those energies, just as with the analysis of returning signals from a radar source. In effect, we map the shape and discontinuities of the building; we can then compare it with some model of what that shape should (?) be.

It is also of importance to understand how buildings behave, depending on whether there is a small or large difference between the interior environmental conditions and those outside. The demands of vernacular housing in the developing countries are an important contrast to those of wealthy users in rich countries: transfer of technology includes the two-way learning processes from these differences.

The clear lesson of building pathology is rather like that of medicine. A great deal can be learnt from studying the dead, but there is also much to be learnt from the living – and it is sometimes more entertaining and encouraging to do so.

Further reading

Anderson, J.M. and Gill, J.R. (1988) *Rainscreen Cladding*, Butterworths, London.

Bravery, A.F., Berry, R.W., Carey, J.K. and Cooper, D.E. (1987) *Recognising Wood Rot and Insect Damage in Buildings*, Department of the Environment/Building Research Establishment, Watford.

Brookes, A.J. and Stacey, M. (1990) Cladding. AJ Focus, *Architects' Journal*, March.

Chadwick, G.F. (1961) *The Works of Sir Joseph Paxton*, Architectural Press, London.

Clifton-Taylor, A. (1972) *The Pattern of English Building*, Faber, London.

Cruickshank, D. and Wyld, P. (1975) *London: The Art of Georgian Building*, Architectural Press, London.

Davey, N. (1961) *A History of Building Materials*, Phoenix House, London.

Davis, G. and Ventre, F. (eds) (1990) *Performance of Buildings and Serviceability of Facilities*, ASTM Special Technical Publication 1029, American Society for Testing and Materials, Philadelphia, Pa.

Hix, J. (1974) *The Glass House*, Phaidon, London.

Institution of Civil Engineers (1985) *Design Life of Buildings*, Thomas Telford, London.

Kohlmaier, G. and von Sartory, B. (1986) *Houses of Glass: A 19th Century Building Type* (1981) (trans. J.C. Harvey) MIT Press, Cambridge, Mass.

Lieff, M. and Trechsel, H.R. (eds) (1982) *Moisture Migration in Buildings*, ASTM Special Technical Publication 779, American Society for Testing and Materials, Philadelphia, Pa.

Masters, L.W. (1987) Service life prediction: a state of the art, in *Fourth International Conference on Durability of Building Materials and Components, Singapore 1987*, Pergamon, Oxford.

Mix, P.E. (1987) *Introduction to Non-destructive Testing*, Wiley, New York.

Saxon, R. (1986) *Atrium Buildings: Development and Design*, 2nd edn, Architectural Press, London.

Seiffert, K. (1970) *Damp Diffusion and Buildings* (trans. A.B. Phillips and F.H. Turner), Elsevier, London.

Spence, R.J.S. and Cook, D.J. (1983) *Building Materials in Developing Countries*, Wiley, Chichester.

CHAPTER SIX

Intelligent buildings and intelligent sites

Since the Honeywell initiatives of the early 1980s, the idea of the **intelligent building**, or **smart building**, to use the American term, has tantalized designers. Broadly speaking, it involves the application of information technology (IT) to the coordination and control of building functions and the machines housed by buildings.

We have seen the beginnings of this electronic automation of buildings in airports, automated warehouses, large libraries (book store recovery, bibliographic searches), supermarkets (with stock control via point-of-sale IT), travel agents, Prestel and Minitel, improved person–person communications (more sophisticated telephone systems, fax, etc.), theatre lighting, robotic factories and the modern workplace generally – especially the modern office.

Although many of these changes will simplify, regularize or otherwise rationalize the workings of buildings, there is no reason to believe either that all such changes will be beneficial or that the central issues of social control are fundamentally new or that new technologies will be any more deterministic than those which have gone before. These concerns will be examined after describing some possible developments. At the same time, it is important that we do not fall into one of two camps: those who believe that the future is a necessary evil; and those who believe it is an *unnecessary* evil.

The intelligent building

The intelligent building programme deals with the application of IT to the many aspects of building design:

- Internal environmental monitoring and control, through the measurement of all flows;
- Safety and security;
- Communications, telecoms and computing;
- In-house appliances and machines;
- Materials handling – receipt, storage, manipulation, dispatch, etc;
- Energy management;
- Active enclosure systems;
- Applications of 'intelligent materials';
- Building records and management, facilities management.

Different building types will be dominated by differing emphases and combinations of these systems. It is interesting to note that already there are two quite distinct sources of these developments: the advanced building industries; and the computer/IT industries. These two can be found in Tokyo, where the Kajima Intelligent Building represents the advanced version of building technologies, whereas the Tron House represents the interest generated out of computer studies of complex systems. The principle of creating an IT matrix for all building functions can be extended to the whole site or even to large urban areas.

The intelligent site

If the necessary IT systems are embedded into and around a site, then it makes possible the systematic enhancement of traditional site infrastructure. This should occur in various ways.

We can expect increased use in all countries of electronic geodesy and monitoring to provide detailed descriptions of the site, including ground, air and water analyses, and their depiction in digitized, multi-dimensional maps. Later developments could include monitoring of energy and matter flows, including pollution, threatening natural disasters, etc.

The framework will evolve for the organization of the building site as a temporary factory, but one which can maximize communications within the site (e.g. robots, measurement, progress assessment, security) and between the site and its operational network (e.g. with the contractor's headquarters, with the client, with suppliers). Some parts of this will affect the 'non-professional' building industries.

We will see more on the development of an intelligent building, phased according to the needs of the client and user and benefitting from successive technical innovations.

The basis and protocols by which the building is tapped into local and wider networks will be enhanced and defined, probably by those manufacturing the hardware.

It may be thought that the presumed extent of such change is exaggerated, that buildings and building sites will not change that quickly. However, during the 1980s, we have seen the rapid proliferation of fax machines, mobile telephones and laser-surveying equipment – and even small modem-linked computers – on building sites in several countries. A large proportion of the population appears to have overcome its reluctance to embrace advanced technology when that comes in the form of work-enhancing 'toys' – appropriately styled.

It may be helpful to recall the impact of small, transistorized radios (which also may be found on building sites). Some analysts even related the rise of nationalism in the late 20th century to this invention: a small broadcasting station, perhaps abroad, can easily reach the urban office worker at her desk or the rural farmer in his field.

The building as a robot

Information technology resulted from the convergence of communications systems, such as telephones, with computers. Telephones were very reliable but not very precise (e.g. distortion of speech). Computers were very precise but not very reliable (e.g. constantly going 'down'). IT combines the merits of both.

Beyond this, however, a computer becomes a robot with systems for sensation, processing and action. Mobility is an extra.

In this sense, buildings have been moving towards the status of robots for some time. They have networks of sensors and these are poised to become extraordinarily more effective, wide-ranging and sensitive. As already noted, microprocessors are

115

being installed in more and more, initially for simple tasks like controlling the central heating. More and more electromechanical devices will become available.

A further dimension of responsive buildings will emerge when they are capable of altering their 'shape' and location more fundamentally than at present. At that point, many will become robots in a more familiar sense. It is worth noting here that the major impact may be in upgradings of existing buildings.

The informating society and concepts of transparency

In her book, *In the Age of the Smart Machine*, Shoshana Zuboff distinguishes between the automating of work in the factory or office and 'informating'. That is, she argues that the effects of information technology on complete work systems are qualitatively quite different from advanced automation. This is because the flows that people examine are now information, not physical flows (such as fluids or paper), and the information is available to everybody. It changes the underlying authority/power structures of the organization, it introduces a certain 'transparency' and hence may induce defensive responses, shields, new reservoirs to maintain monitoring/control of the information flow and the flow of instructions.

She takes the analysis a stage further in a convincing analysis of the work of the French historian, Michel Foucault, and his work on institutional buildings such as prisons. Foucault has drawn attention to the work of the English philosopher Jeremy Bentham and his proposals for a Panopticon, a building so designed that those in charge could see and control all the prisoners from a single central position (Fig. 7). The building he designed, a version of which was built by his engineer brother Samuel in 1787, involved a central plan and extensive use of iron frames sheathed in glass. This produced what Bentham called 'universal transparency'.

Foucault comments that this 'Visibility is a trap . . . Each individual, in his place, is securely confined . . . He is seen, but he does not see; he is the object of information, never a subject in communication'. Architectural historians (e.g. Anthony Vidler), have found Foucault's work crucial in understanding the forms and intentions of 18th century buildings, through his studies of the

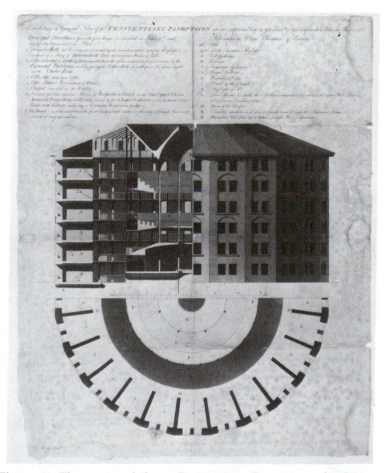

Figure 7 The proposal for a Penitentiary Panopticon, by Jeremy Bentham. This was a version of his concept of the Inspection House, with its central surveillance position and its generation from three precepts: Mercy; Justice; Vigilance.

modern relationships between power, knowledge and institutional forms. Zuboff draws a parallel between this form of architectural transparency and control, and the pursuit of its modern equivalent through information technologies.

Three points arise here. First, it is plain that information technology is introduced into buildings to achieve better control of

117

the flows of people, matter and energy. The preoccupations with security (controlling flows of people by name, status, time and place), safety, and environmental control make this clear. The 'social transparency' of buildings will become a major area of building analysis.

Figure 8 Urban block: buildings in Bilbao, Spain. Note the use of a glazed volume outside the door/windows of the buildings. This enables a complex control system of solar radiation, heat loss, ventilation, etc.

118

Figure 9 Seaside block: building on the North Spanish coast. Note the complex system of glazed and open balconies, providing control of wind, solar radiation, heat loss, etc.

Secondly, the analysis of whole building information systems will become an important tool in understanding how buildings operate in many other ways, as responsive systems in unstable equilibrium. The infrastructure foundations of the 'intelligent site' will form the initial matrix of that system.

Thirdly, the issue of transparency remains a major point of technical development in building enclosures (Figs 8 and 9). New ideas about the use of glass in buildings suggest that we will build much more on the ability of glass to act as a filter of specified wavelengths of electromagnetic radiation. With new coatings, glass panels will become comprehensive filters and emitters of a whole variety of controlled radiations, whether visible or not. Together with entrapped air, or even vacuum voids, they will form complex layered enclosure systems.

The residual worry about the use of information technologies must be that they are presented as neutral, as simple tools.

However, unlike earlier tools, they are able to measure and evaluate the activity of those using them. If we extend this proposition to whole buildings, then we will have to think very carefully about the ways in which buildings are managed and how concepts of 'data protection' can be amplified. The power of the techniques is fascinating, as is their potential for transforming some aspects of building operations, but, like most tools, they can also be weapons.

Further reading

Ando, M. and Groák, S. (eds) (1990) *Habitat International*, **14**, 2–3, Special issue on the UK–Japan Construction Research Seminar, University College London see especially J. Powell, Intelligent design teams design intelligent buildings.

Brookes, A.J. and Stacey, M. (1991) Glazing and curtain walling. AJ Focus, *Architects' Journal*, April.

Building IT 2000, The Building Centre Trust, London, 1991.

Button, D.A. and Dunning, R. (1989) *Fenestration 2000*, Pilkington Glass Ltd, St Helens, July.

Brown, M.A. (1989) *The Application of Robotics and Advanced Automation to the Construction Industry*, CIOB Occasional Paper No. 38, Chartered Institute of Building, Ascot, April.

Eyke, M. (1988) *Building Automation Systems*, Blackwell, Oxford.

Foucault, M. (1975) *Discipline and Punish: The Birth of the Prison* (trans. A. Sheridan), Allen Lane, London.

Gann, D.M. (1991) Buildings for the Japanese information economy. *Futures*, June, 469–81.

Kohlmaier, G. and von Sartory, B. (1986) *Houses of Glass: A 19th Century Building Type* (1981) (trans. J.C. Harvey), MIT Press, Cambridge, Mass.

Koolhaas, R. (1978) *Delirious New York*, Oxford University Press, New York.

Kroner, W.M. (1989) The new frontier: intelligent architecture through intelligent design. *Futures*, August, 319–33.

National Economic Development Office (NEDO) (1987) *Pathfinding Report on the Security Equipment Industry*, NEDO, London.

Newstead, A. (1989) Future information cities. *Futures*, June, 263–76.

Paulson, B.C. (1985) Automation and robotics for construction, *Journal of Construction Engineering and Management*, ASCE, **111**(3), September.

Robins, K. and Hepworth, M. (1988) Electronic spaces: new technologies and the future of cities. *Futures*, April, 155–76.

Rowe, C. (1976) *The Mathematics of the Ideal Villa and Other Essays*, MIT Press, Cambridge, Mass; see especially (with R. Slutzky) Transparency: literal and phenomenal.

Vidler, A. (1987) *The Writing of the Walls*, Princeton Architectural Press, Princeton, NJ.

Zuboff, S. (1988) *In the Age of the Smart Machine*, Basic Books, New York.

CHAPTER SEVEN

The building process

Buildings are the result of industrial and social processes. Today we are more conscious than ever of the significance of the distinct 'building process' and its situation within the broader development process. It dominates our understanding of 'the building industry', which is often seen as the sum total of thousands of separate building processes across a country.

In very general terms, the building process may be defined as the organizing or bringing together of a set of inputs or resource flows, and their assembly or transformation into a specified building output or product, in a given period of time, on a specified site.

In its simplest practical form, the building process involves a client or owner, who requires a building and commissions a building team. Someone designs or specifies the building arrangement and construction, often an architect, supported by other consultants such as structural and services engineers. Someone recovers materials, manufactures components. Someone (such as the building contractor) constructs the building from these materials and components in accordance with the specification. It is then occupied and used, after which further building works may be required. This pattern has evolved over centuries. Today these various roles and relationships are experiencing their most vigorous rearrangement and redefinition.

All of these activities can be analysed in terms of the building process. To understand the building process, and the building industry more generally, it is necessary to examine what resources are actually used, how they are transformed, and what are the different roles or occupations of the people concerned with the production of buildings. Process and product are intimately linked, in ways which are different from most other forms of manufacturing or service industry. During the past forty years or so, the very idea of 'the building process' has itself affected the behaviours and perceptions of that industry.

The idea of process has been reflected in two ways. First, it has provided a basic framework for many studies of the industrial structure, particularly where linkages have been sought with other sectors of national economies. Secondly, they have affected the evolution of various forms of contract and hence the reality of the role and responsibilities of many participants (such as the quantity surveying profession in the UK). In the case of the UK (and other countries whose building industry procedures have been modelled on the UK), the adversarial structure which permeates the UK legal, political and public administrative systems has given rise to extraordinarily strong professions – in the building industry and elsewhere. These, in turn, have greatly specialized. These factors must be borne in mind when analysing the central model of the building process presented here.

Inputs to the building process

The inputs to the building process involve two types of resources. There are those which are 'consumed', which are permanently used up in producing the building, termed **circulating capital** by economists. And there are those which are utilized for all or part of the process, whose time is 'consumed', termed **fixed capital**. The resources we use include:

- Land;
- Existing building stock and infrastructure;
- Materials and components;
- Energy and fuel;
- Manpower;
- Machines, plant and tools;
- Finance.

These are examined further, because some apparently simple and obvious facts about the building process lead to sometimes surprising characteristics of the building industry.

'Buy land', said Mark Twain, 'they ain't making it any more'. Whether as commodity or as capital, land provides the sites to which, for the most part, buildings are fixed. That buildings are fixed to the ground means that we have to have a mobile industry, an industry which creates a temporary factory to which materials, machines and people are transported. It means that for each project a unique pattern of linkages with materials suppliers and component manufacturers has to be established for all the flows. The common workplace for the assembly of the building leads to a series of confusions characteristic of this process.

Existing constructions – buildings, works and infrastructure – may form a crucial matrix into which this temporary factory is embedded. Buckminster Fuller once suggested that buildings are merely nozzles on the urban infrastructure; in some countries we might now think of them as terminals on the global information network. The pattern of existing services and buildings may define many features of the building and even the organization of the site as a factory.

During the 19th century, factory production of building components developed rapidly in Europe and North America. Buildings and the processes changed as designers and constructors in industrialized countries were able to draw increasingly upon off-the-shelf components. Some examples are instructive.

The Georgian and Victorian builders of a rapidly growing London, as Britain urbanized with the drive of its Industrial Revolution, developed a new model of the general builder, linked to the use of standard house designs and standardized factory components (doors, windows, staircases, decorative features, etc.). In the USA, as part of the development westwards, a method of prefabricated timber housing was devised which could be transported by railway.

One of the defining buildings of this approach to **component building** was the Crystal Palace, with its use of factory-made iron, timber and glass components. What was more significant was the concept of the building process inherent in the project, the relationship between site assembly and factory production. Related developments included the prefabricated hospitals for the Crimean War – the first 'industrial war' – and the astonishing precision of the Eiffel Tower.

The building materials industry today compares in size with the building industry in most developed countries; and its role is regarded as critical in many poorer countries, to prevent a devastating dependence on imported building products. There is an extraordinary array of suppliers of materials – such as cement, timber, bricks, thermal insulants, impervious membranes, etc. – and manufacturers of components – such as window–wall assemblies, roof trusses, radiators and boilers, switches and cabling, door and window furniture, etc. Strongly linked with these firms are a further array of specialist fabricators, of structural steelwork, pipework and ductwork of various forms, etc.

This extensive system of factory-produced materials and components has changed the building process out of all recognition. Designers can assume the availability of off-the-shelf components; they can also assume the availability of special variations from those factories, based upon the stock designs and expert manufacturing advice. (Implicitly, this is part of a redefinition of the 'designer' in the building industry.) The result has been a tendency to greater use of prefabricated components, standardization of construction and the development of 'work packages' – distinct elements of the building designed to suit a given subcontractor/manufacturer.

For building processes, energy has three principal dimensions. First, energy and fuel are used in the manufacture of the machines by which materials and components are produced. Secondly, considerable energy may be used in the actual production of components and materials – e.g. the manufacture of cement or aluminium. We are only now beginning to recognize the full environmental impact of these production methods. Thirdly, the assembly phase of construction involves machines (to excavate and dig, to transport materials, to lift components into position) and powered hand-tools (to cut, to drill, to shape materials, to fix one component to another).

The broad heading of manpower includes:

- Initiators and users – private owners/clients, public sector organizations, developers, user representatives, etc;
- Professions – architects, engineers, quantity surveyors (in some countries) or other cost consultants, project managers, work planners, estimators, constructors, etc. – concerned with design, specification, organization and planning; these often work in offices;

- Operatives – skilled craftsmen, semi-skilled trades, unskilled operatives; these usually work in factories and on site; new demands for maintenance expertise are emerging;
- Management – procurement, finance, specification, cost, time, design offices, factory production, site organization, etc;
- Monitoring and quality control – statutory controls, progress, health and safety, compliance with contract requirements – e.g. via Clerks of Works (in some countries), etc.

Tools have always represented technologies, as reified know-how. Over the past forty years or so, a major development has been in the machines available to building contractors. Plant hire has also meant that even small contractors have access to large modern and sophisticated equipment. Partly through encouragement from the home-owner DIY markets, there has been extraordinary growth in the provision of powered hand-tools – associated with highly sophisticated fixing devices for pre-finished components.

This vast repertory of machines represents a form of built-in know-how, a means by which the building process switches its emphasis from circulating capital to fixed capital. It has also raised issues of appropriate technologies in building, especially in poorer countries where cheap labour is readily available and where building processes offer not only employment, but training in a variety of skills.

More recently, there has been considerable impact of information technology (IT) on the building process. The most obvious machine presence has been the use of computers in design offices, in cost analysis, in contractors' planning offices and in organizing wages. The expectation must be that such machines will vastly expand the access to documented and feedback know-how in specifying both design and production methods, especially in large projects. With increased sophistication of image-processing and fast access to large databases, computer-aided design (CAD) is making rapid inroads into ordinary practice.

Finance for building projects is a large topic in its own right. It is needed to animate every phase of the building process, from initial procurement, to providing liquidity for the offices and organizations, to providing working capital for the contractor. The significant change in the past thirty years has been the level of interest rates, combined with the role of the property markets, which has provided a major pressure for rapid project methods.

Building as a product or output

Italian architect Duccio Turin identified typical features of conventional buildings as products, whose characteristics have a major effect on the nature of the building industry:

- Fixity – i.e. a building is usually fixed to a particular site. So part of the industry will always have to be mobile to assemble it there;
- Uniqueness – each building is a unique project on a unique site. Each building project has therefore to be organized distinctly, even if part of a larger contract;
- Weight. Buildings use heavy but cheap materials, with implications that these cannot be transported very great distances;
- Bulk or volume. This follows from people's space needs;
- Complexity of organization and manufacture;
- Long production time, compared to most other manufacturing. Combined with the above features, this means a special organization for producing each contract;
- High initial and running costs. Combined with the above features, this has led to very complex finance methods;
- Longevity of use. This is related also to finance methods. Different elements and components have differing useful lifetimes, but the basic structure and fabric are expected to last several decades;
- Often sold before built, in distinction to most manufactured products. Speculative building, of course, does not quite conform to this notion.

Attempts to rationalize or improve the efficiency of the building industry have often involved changing at least one of these features, often driven by perceived relative scarcity of one or more of the resources listed above.

For instance, if buildings are usually fixed to the ground, what happens if they become 'mobile'? Experience in the USA from the 1930s onwards has shown some useful lessons in two forms: properly mobile homes, which can move at will; and 'one-time' mobile homes, which move once – from factory to site.

If they are unique and complex, what happens if we try to standardize them? If they are heavy and bulky, what happens if we seek to shrink and lighten them? In many countries after the Second World War, shortages of strategic materials and skilled labour led to arguments for lighter construction and less uniqueness (greater standardization).

If buildings take a long time to produce, what happens if we accelerate their production? In recent years, in countries with high interest rates, this has been a major issue since faster construction should have major financial benefits.

If buildings normally last a long time, what happens if we assume a short life? Will it affect the technologies used? Will it affect finance methods? In poor countries, where short-lived construction has often been the reality, it means constant renewal work on the buildings. In rich countries we now find that the amortization period for some urban commercial buildings may be under ten years, after which they have zero asset value and can be demolished: part of the argument here also is that such buildings are highly dependent upon the modern IT office technology, whose rapid changes often require major changes to the buildings relatively quickly.

Above all, these features have meant a project-based building industry which has to be mobile and which often has to wait upon clients to define what work is to be carried out. This need to be a responsive industry, rather than an initiating industry, has been thought to restrict its ability to invest in new methods and machines. This perception greatly influenced the thinking of central governments in many countries during the 1950s and 1960s, as they sought industrial development policies – often within national planning frameworks.

Transformation, production and the building team

The organizations principally involved in the building process, as reflected in the professional building industry, work in offices, in factories, and on the building site – the 'temporary factory'. The main participants concerned, who are broadly identified above under 'manpower', fulfil an extraordinary wide range of occupations and roles – more of them perhaps informal than formal.

The organizational structure of even large design offices,

together with those of the associated consultants, is usually relatively simple. The necessary personal qualifications have tended to be tightly defined (e.g. by professional institutions in some countries). The functions have been fairly constant. By contrast, contracting organizations above a certain size are more complex, employing a wider range of skills and fulfilling many different functions for the central organization and the on-site contracts. The organization of manufacturers and other off-site production is more recognizable to analysts from other industries and depends upon the size of the firm, range of its markets and products, etc. We can anticipate that the organization of design and contractors' firms will change significantly in the future as the building process volatilizes and the design expertise in building technologies disperses.

The overriding characteristic of the building team is that it is formed from a nesting series of temporary coalitions of people and organizations. There are two principal causes. First, the co-ordinating team for design and production – architect, engineers, other consultants, a contractor – are probably working together for the first time; even if the employing organizations have collaborated before, the actual people carrying out the work will most likely be new to one another. If we add in the fact that only a few clients commission more than one building, the critical point is emphasized.

Secondly, the most difficult aspect of the building process to describe satisfactorily is the organization of the building site, the focus of the process. Although the use of subcontractors is well known in building, in the UK and other countries during the 1970s and 1980s there has been a major increase in the division of labour and greatly increased use of specialist sub-contractors, labour-only subcontractors, etc. This has exacerbated the problem of coordinating the many different trade gangs on site, many of whom will visit the site for only a small part of the total contract period. It is clear that not only are there fundamentally distinct versions of the building process, in the sense of contractual combinations of the main participants, but that within any given contract there is great volatility of organization, especially on site. Indeed, if we 'froze' the site organization suddenly at a moment, we would probably be very surprised to discover exactly what local organization was prevailing at that moment.

Variety of building process

A final reflection on the plethora of building processes with which we have to contend. Different sub-markets may draw upon quite distinct resources, resources which are not inter-changeable. We may therefore speak of building *industries* (plural), to make plain that some building markets involve fundamentally different systems of building processes. Economic and technological change may proceed in completely different ways in each sub-market. For instance, the building methods used by volume housebuilders are quite distinct from those used by constructors of modern 'clean technology' factories. These markets may fragment further, making it even more important for us to understand clearly how such temporary and partitioned processes can operate as effectively as they do.

Further reading

Briggs, M.S. (1945) *A Short History of the Building Crafts*, Oxford University Press, Oxford.

Fitchen, J. (1986) *Building Construction before Mechanisation*, MIT Press, Cambridge, Mass.

Groák, S. (1983) Building processes and technological choice. *Habitat International*, **7**, 5–6, 357–366.

Groák, S. and Ive, G. (1986) Economics and technological change: some implications for the study of the building industry. *Habitat International*, **10**, 4, 115–32.

Harper, D.R. (1990) *Building: The Process and the Product* (1978), Chartered Institute of Building, Ascot.

Hillebrandt, P.M. (1984) *Analysis of the British Construction Industry*, Macmillan, London.

Ive, G. (1983) *Capacity and Response to Demand of the Housebuilding Industry*. Building Economics Research Unit, University College London.

Ive, G. and McGhie, W.J. (1983) The relation of construction to other industries, *Production of the Built Environment*, **4**.

Koenigsberger, O.H. and Groák, S. (eds) (1978) *Essays in Memory of Duccio Turin*, Pergamon, Oxford.

Oxley, R. and Poskitt, J. (1986) *Management Techniques Applied to the Construction Industry*, 4th edn, Collins, London.

Richardson, H.W. and Aldcroft, D.H. (1968) *Building in the British Economy between the Wars*, Allen and Unwin, London.

CHAPTER EIGHT

Systems and conventions

The Argentinean librarian J.L. Borges once invoked a probably fictional Chinese encyclopedia, in which it is written that animals are classified as:

- belonging to the Emperor
- embalmed
- tame
- sucking pigs
- sirens
- fabulous
- stray dogs
- included in the present classification
- frenzied
- innumerable
- drawn with a very fine camel-hair brush
- *et cetera*
- having just broken the water pitcher
- that from a long way off look like flies

Although startling, this classification is instructive. First of all, it works. We could go out into the world and classify those animals we encounter according to this system. Secondly, it reminds us that any classification system has an underlying style, something it wishes to convey. It is not objective or neutral. It may even imply a theoretical framework. Thirdly, the encyclopedia makes clear that there is a set of categories which define what elements are part of a system and what are outside it altogether. Similar considerations arise in the arrangement of building systems.

As building methods have developed, designers and constructors have sought to systematize their work, to divide the labour and improve the skills and methods by specialization, to benefit from repetition of well-tried solutions. This has sometimes been associated with attempts to reduce the proportion of building work carried out on site, confined as it is by weather and space.

The systems approach to building starts from observation of our own actions over time. Every building project is unique and, to an extent, every building is unique. However, we do not design every building anew, without reference to previous experiences. Although we may use building materials in new combinations, the palette of materials, jointing methods and components from which we select is both limited and – increasingly – repetitive. Although every site is organized uniquely, the practical problems of making the building fall into familiar patterns.

It is rather like our knowledge of language, where, once we have learnt to speak, we are able to construct or understand sentences which have never occurred before, even if we prefer clichés or are baffled by too much novelty.

Today, we can recognize two distinct notions of system building, which overlap with concepts of 'industrialization', 'prefabrication' and 'standardization'. One of them emerges from a contractor-led model of the building process; the other is generated more out of a manufacturer-led model.

Process approach

The first has been the use of standard buildings, perhaps in sets of half-a-dozen or so variations. Many of the major house-building systems used in the USA over the past sixty years take this form. It could also be argued that many rural vernacular houses around the world fall into this category. And a significant proportion of industrial and agricultural buildings have used such an approach.

The overall organization and shape of the building is fixed, but variations of specific components may be encouraged through competition based on specifications. There is no attempt to enable different configurations of the same components. This version of system building is dominated by the assembly organization.

Two impressive examples of such an approach have existed for more than fifty years. They are the Wimpey 'No Fines' system in the UK, and the Levitt system in the USA. Both are industrialized housing systems. But we can see precursors of this approach in the urban development systems of the UK in the late 18th and 19th centuries, as the idea of the 'contractor' emerged, alongside the use of off-site works for specific components (e.g. door-sets, windows, decorative features in Coade stone and other artificial materials).

The development of this form of system building is based on the organization of the process, drawing on production analyses from advanced manufacturing and dominated by the client organization. Some of the most interesting developments in the 1970s and 1980s have been associated with the evolution of the 'professional client' – the client or client organization which can take a continuous technical role in the building process. It may be the speculative builder.

This development has received considerable attention in the 1980s, although it has not been formally recognized as a type of industrialized or system building. It seeks, amongst other things, to overcome the conflicts of other kinds of building process. Despite the attention to building as a communications system, considerable mismatches have occurred. This is because the building process in many industrialized countries has been predicated on an adversarial approach following the endemic conflict which (perfectly properly) exists between parties with genuinely different interests and commitments. The approach seeks to minimize technical and programme defects by changing the structure of communication and responsibility.

Component buildings

Today we have naming of parts. Yesterday,
We had daily cleaning. And tomorrow morning,
We shall have what to do after firing. But today,
Today we have naming of parts. Japonica
Glistens like coral in all of the neighbouring gardens,
       And today we have naming of parts.

They call it easing the Spring: it is perfectly easy
If you have any strength in your thumb: like the bolt,

And the breech, and the cocking-piece, and the point of
balance,
Which in our case we have not got; and the almond-
blossom
Silent in all of the gardens and the bees going backwards
and forwards,
For today we have naming of parts.

from Lessons of the War,
Henry Reed, c.1946

The second form of industrialization is dominated by the manufacturers of building components, sometimes working closely
with designers.

Some components have been standardized over centuries –
such as bricks and tiles – and there exists an enticing set of myths
to justify each standard. The use of modular frameworks has
existed for centuries – e.g. in Europe since the early Renaissance.
However, the real drive to combine standardization with systematic building grew with the development of the off-site fabrication
shops and the factory-based building component industry.

As site work became increasingly concerned with assembly of
components, rather than the shaping and jointing of materials,
the idea emerged of building from a 'kit of parts'. Once this
was explicitly formulated, it became clear that its successful
operation depended on four interrelated 'rules of engagement' or
conventions:

- The proportional systems and geometries of architectural
  composition;
- The dimensional coordination of different components and
  materials – often on the basis of a three-dimensional rectilinear
  grid and a standard modular dimension;
- The methods of jointing material to material or component to
  component, whether a repeat or different;
- The production and assembly tolerances involved.

These had to be agreed conventions within a given kit of parts,
or building system, for those parts to be compatible and inter-
changeable, depending on what arrangement of components
was desired. If the rules were particular to one kit of parts, this
was regarded as a **closed system** since parts from another kit
would not fit within it. Such a kit or system might be developed

by one organization – e.g. the prefabricated systems of school building developed after the Second World War in the UK, and subsequently in California, USA. If the rules were shared amongst many kits of parts, or applied still more widely to a range of otherwise unrelated components, then this was described as an **open system**. Independent products not controlled by a central organization could be exchanged for those products made deliberately for the system.

This concept of building, which was also known as 'the component approach', has achieved a distinction in what have come to be called 'hi-tech' buildings. In the 1960s the wonderful confections and wicked insights of the Archigram Group in London introduced clear images of the technologies needed for 'plug-in' buildings and even 'walking cities'.

Behind the assumptions, however, to this day, have been realities of manufacturing production for established systems, where the manufacturer had to wait on orders via the general contractors. For some time, there were issues of how long a run could economically be provided, what were the inventory costs of components for stock, how long was the set-up time for new components, to what extent could manufacturers rely on predictions or even promises of orders, what was the capacity utilization of the production plant, and so on. Many of these factors meant that supposed economies of scale were rarely realized, although better prices through bulk buying were achieved.

It is of interest to explore the new procedures of 'just in time' production, eliminating inventory and multiple-handling costs, to see whether they will change the balance of trade between manufacturers and assemblers of building components.

This confluence of industrialization methods appears to mean that we are seeing the last of the traditional structures of the building trade, as more and more of the control in the industry reorganizes four sectors – the client organizations, the manufacturers, the designer/specifiers, the assemblers. One of the fascinating aspects of these developments will be to see whose existing methods and meanings come to dominate the building processes of the future.

Further reading

Ball, M. (1988) *Rebuilding Construction*, Routledge, London.

Banham, R. (1981) *Design by Choice* (ed. P. Sparke), Academy Editions, London.

Bignell, V., Dooner, M., Hughes, L., Pym, C. and Stone, S. (eds) (1985) *Manufacturing Systems: Context, Applications and Techniques*, Basil Blackwell, Oxford.

Bowley, M. (1966) *The British Building Industry: Four Studies in Change*, Cambridge University Press, Cambridge.

Buffa, E.S. (1983) *Modern Production/Operations Management*, Wiley, New York.

Cook, P. (1970) *Experimental Architecture*, Universe Books, New York.

Cruickshank, D. and Wyld, P. (1975) *London: The Art of Georgian Building*, Architectural Press, London.

Drewer, S.P. (1990) The international construction system. *Habitat International*, **14**, 2–3 (in press).

Dunster, D. (1990) Collaboration in education: the Diploma project at the Bartlett School, 1988–89. *Journal of Architectural Education*, **43**, 2, Winter, 14–21.

Ehrenkrantz, E.D. (1989) *Architectural Systems: A Needs, Resources and Design Approach*, McGraw-Hill, New York.

Foster, N. (ed.) (1969) Town workshop. *Architectural Review*; Special issue, November.

Groák, S. (1984) The undecorated shed and its attic. *Building with Steel*, 18, September, 10–15.

Groák, S. (1985) A Cambridge test: Hopkins for Schlumberger. *Architects' Journal*, 18, September, 43–56.

Harriss, J. (1976) *The Eiffel Tower*, Elek, London; first published, 1975, *The Tallest Tower*, Mifflin, New York.

Hobhouse, H. (1971) *Thomas Cubitt – Master Builder*, Macmillan, London.

Huber, B. and Steinegger, J.-C. (eds) (1971) *Jean Prouvé*, Artemis, Zurich.

Russell, B. (1981) *Building Systems, Industrialisation and Architecture*, Wiley, London.

Saint, A. (1987) *Towards a Social Architecture*, Yale University Press, London.

Sugden, D. (ed.) (1968) The anatomy of the factory. *Architectural Design*, Special issue, November.

Turin, D.A. (ed.) (1965) *Housing in Africa*, Document E/CN/14/HOU/7/Rev., United Nations, New York, September.

Turin, D.A. (1967–8) Building as a process. *Transactions of the Bartlett Society*, **6**, 83–108.

Wachsmann, K. (1961) *The Turning Point of Building* (trans. T.E. Burton), Reinhold, New York.

Wells, J. (1986) *The Construction Industry in Developing Countries: Alternative Strategies for Development*, Croom Helm, London.

White, R.B. (1965) *Prefabrication: A History of its Development in Great Britain*, HMSO, London.

CHAPTER NINE

What industry follows function?

If the problem of the dwelling or the flat were studied in the same way that a chassis is, a speedy transformation and improvement would be seen in our houses. If houses were constructed by industrial mass-production, like chassis, unexpected but sane and defensible forms would soon appear, and a new aesthetic would be formulated with astonishing precision.

Le Corbusier, 1927

I think that cars today are almost the exact equivalent of the great Gothic cathedrals: I mean the supreme creation of an era, conceived with passion by unknown artists, and consumed in image if not in usage by a whole population which appropriates them as a magical object.

Roland Barthes, 1957

The comparison is often made between the building industry and the car industry, usually to suggest that we should be able to transfer the production methods of the automobile assembly line – as popularized through the original Ford Model T – to transform our methods of building (especially housing). The clearest version of this approach was developed in the 1920s and 1930s, in the USA, by Albert Farwell Bemis and strongly affected ideas of dimensional coordination in building.

This interest in the car analogy has plainly arisen with the emergence of the building materials industries and the building component industries. It probably appealed to those who prefer walking around a warm, dry factory to struggling across a building site on a cold, damp evening. It is a way of describing buildings as manufactured objects: machines of this kind have shown an astonishing capacity for transforming people's lives.

Despite the fact that cars can be sold for around ten times as much as houses, on cost per square metre of usable floor space, there has been a constant assumption that they can be equated and therefore that we should transfer work from the house-building site into factories. So we have seen the evolution of mobile homes (caravans, etc.) and one-time mobile houses – transferred by vehicle from factory to site – sometimes in large segments.

This conception of the **building production line** has fed both the rhetoric of function in the building industry and the ways in which the public at large evaluate buildings in use. This is because once the building is regarded as a repetitive object, and the concept of 'type' in architectural history is relevant here, function is one of the categories by which it can be analysed: people use buildings, work in them, congregate in them, in generalizable activities susceptible to functional analysis, whether in the language of work study or in the language of social ritual.

But further: the language of architecture, of building is – in some literal fashion – that of construction, of specification. These are the words which have meaning throughout the industry, which have legal force, which define the quality and quantity of what is to be built. As we change the basis of specification, we change what has meaning in the industry. This chapter explores some of the meanings and metaphors which have fed our concepts of the nature of the building industry itself.

Function

We use the term **functional** in many different ways. We refer to a functional design as one which seems well suited to its purpose, although that may be short-lived. We describe 'functionalist' buildings, those in which the principal volumes are identified with principal functions of the occupying organization – e.g. a factory (with its warehousing, production line, clerical sections, senior managers, etc.). Similarly, we use the word to classify buildings where the central activity is on public display, such as the recent building for the *Financial Times* in London, in which the printing presses are prominently visible to the passer-by. Curiously, we also use 'functionalist' as building abuse, as a way of saying that the building belongs to a failed category. We are suffering from function fatigue. In effect, the word has outlived its useful life of precision and evocation. What will join or replace it?

Our use of terms like function is also bound up with metaphors from nature, beliefs that the natural world has solved all problems of functional efficiency. In thinking this way, we sometimes overlook the effect of time and changing environments, the process of evolution. This may be illustrated by a plea in *New Scientist* magazine from Derek Ager:

> It really is a pity about the panda, but it is a most inefficient animal . . . it is essentially a herbivore designed as a carnivore.
>
> The panda's front teeth are those of a normal flesh-eater, but its back teeth are flattened to grind its vegetable diet . . . the greater part of what it eats passes straight through its system without being digested.
>
> The creature has poor eyesight, poor hearing and a poor sense of smell. It will eat small mammals (and the BBC says that it can be tempted with pork chops), but it is too slow-moving to hunt. The females can become pregnant on only about three days a year . . . The babies are very small and vulnerable when born and it is a long time before they can walk.
>
> Pandas are restricted to a small mountainous area in southwestern China, at about 3000 metres, and will tolerate only such intermediate climates . . . pandas were stranded here when the more efficient carnivores made use of the abundant prey lower down.
>
> As a palaeontologist I know of many thousands of animals that have become extinct, including many that were probably much more efficient than the panda . . . I feel tempted to say 'Let it go . . .'

This sorry tale reminds us that forms of construction have been and gone, sometimes to return. As UK builder Michael Hatchett has argued, particular methods emerge, become refined and developed, decline as their prominence is overtaken by events.

The evolution of the medieval scarf-joint in English timber construction is a good example, reaching the peak of its functional efficiency in the 13th and 14 centuries. Once other methods of creating longer spans in timber from more than one piece of wood were developed (e.g. trusses), it could not maintain its dominant position in the construction repertory.

Furthermore, if we persist in a completely functionalist analysis, without reference to evolution, we then find it very difficult to explain any form of change at all. There is a place for everything, and everything is in its place.

Function is not only a measure of usefulness at the time. The term itself changes meaning and use.

One concept which has evolved from function to take a major place in the language of the building industry is 'performance'. It provides a lucid link between the work of the building industry and that of the building materials industries.

The performance approach

One of the most important developments in building research has been the **performance approach**. This framework is the attempt to define buildings and their constituent parts in terms of what performance-in-use they should achieve over time. It is distinct from defining what we require, either in terms of known solutions or in terms of general function.

For instance, thermal performance might be defined in terms of a stipulated minimum loss of energy from the whole building over a defined period, as compared to a *functional* requirement that the building be designed to achieve 'energy efficiency', as compared to a specific design *solution* (e.g. provide 50 mm of extruded polystyrene cavity insulation to a given specification).

The approach is intended to define exactly what we require the eventual product to do, in definable and measurable terms. It is intended as a framework to enable systematic innovation, in which new or more cost-effective solutions may emerge provided they still satisfy our requirements.

In practice, it has been borrowed from mechanical engineering to help in the purchase of components and systems for buildings from competing manufacturers and other suppliers or subcontractors. It thus provides the bridge between the specification of buildings and the specification of components, in a manner which is supposedly not prejudiced to any one solution.

It has become the convention that we invoke six principal characteristics of the performance approach to ensure that all those bidding will do so on a common basis, so that in principle we can 'compare like with like' at the level of performance:

- We must define the terminology to be use (e.g. as in specified standards), so that those responding to the request for a building product know what is intended when certain words are used;
- We have to list performance requirements – what the product is to achieve in use – in assessable terms;
- We have to define the service conditions or environment in which the building or elements are placed;
- We have to define what criteria will be used to determine acceptance or rejection of proposals, in ways which relate to the performance requirements;
- We must evaluate in terms of agreed data – nature, units, format and timing;
- We must identify what will be the methods of assessment and verification.

Whether mindless or reasonable, certain limitations of the approach are apparent. First, we are not able always to specify with precision all of the performance attributes we require. Even if we try to extrapolate from known solutions, we have difficulty in that we do not invariably know all of their successful qualities. The method favours those attributes which can be calculated. Secondly, we have requirements of buildings which cannot be expressed in terms of measurable performance – e.g. aesthetic appearance or social appropriateness. Thirdly, the approach implies a systematic sequence of design and production which may not always exist. Finally, it is aggregative, it sums the achievements by separate category; it is not easily adaptable to holistic descriptions.

That said, the benefit of the approach is that it encourages a greater explicitness and provides an initial helpful framework when we are confronted with problems for which we do not have suitable precedents or existing general solutions. But it only goes so far: the power of the idea is to ask: 'Just what is it that buildings do do? What might they do? What would you like them to do?' As we begin to answer, we crash straight into the many uncertainties and ambiguities described in Book One, notably the questions of how we even describe the industry itself, and how we define and measure 'whole building performance'.

What kind of industry is the building industry?

The many and various versions of purpose, use, function and performance are related to some picture of what kind of industry we now believe the building industry to be.

It is often assumed that the building industry is a version of manufacturing. Although it depends increasingly on the manufacturing industries for materials and components, it is better understood in terms of assembly on a given site (like shipbuilding? or the aircraft industry?), or services (like hospitals? or catering?), temporary coalitions (like the tourist industry?) Or is it really just a network and a set of lists, like the telephone directory: too many characters and no plot?

An English engineer, Peter Ross, has drawn an interesting parallel between managing the organization of a building project and making a movie film: each needs both a director and a producer, to fulfil different managerial purposes. I take this analogy further.

The movie industry forms a new coalition of people, organizations, skills, information, purposes, equipment, etc. for each major film. It has parallel organizations for the production of TV soap operas, documentaries, science series about the natural world, animations, computer videos, and so on. Home movies and videos also have their own economic, technical and organizational structures. In each case, it is possible to define the project as the organizational core.

The allegiances of those working on movies vary, sometimes based on public demand, sometimes on trade/craft guilds. The organizational and contractual allegiances appear (at least to this outsider) rather reminiscent of the building industry. The film industry employs significant numbers of building craftsmen – e.g. many of the best plasterers from the building industry are busy constructing sets. As one of Agatha Christie's detectives remarks, investigating a murder which happened during a home theatrical production: 'Theatre may involve the creation of illusion, but the sets are real – they are made of real wood, real cloth, real paint . . .'

There may or may not be major 'stars', but a multitude of others are involved. Occasionally, there are demands for historical accuracy and authenticity, the benefits of nostalgia, the projection of possible futures. The site may be a studio set or a 'real' location. It appears that there is still an argument about whether film is an art form. It is no accident that so many important film directors have previously trained in architecture.

The analogy persists in social psychology: there have been provocative proposals that we would understand people's behaviour in buildings better, and hence design more suitable environments, if we treated them as acting out social situations in 'sets', with 'props'.

What comes out of these comparisons? That we must identify many different industries within the building industry, some written one over another as time passes – but retaining traces of their former glories, palimpsests.

The organization of building work

I propose to identify three ways of organizing building work in a social context. The first I call the **formal sector**, or professional full-time industry. This involves legally constituted firms of designers, consultants and building contractors, etc. Building teams are organized for each contract, sometimes involving separate design teams and production teams. The work is explicitly subject to statutory controls, standards and conditions of employment; it is scrutinized accordingly. Although dominated by private companies, in some countries there may be a significant level of publicly owned building organizations (sometimes called 'direct labour'). It is this visible range of activities which is usually meant when people speak of 'the building industry'.

The formal sector includes a substantial amount of small works; these will usually be produced by the small contracting firms which dominate – by number, rather than by workload – a typical modern building industry. At the other end of the spectrum, we find huge and sophisticated construction activities, at the scale of whole towns, requiring decades of work (i.e. 'macroprojects'). By the time they are complete, people sometimes wonder why they

143

started. But the process is significant: very large contractors operating on the international market have grown in importance. There is reason to believe that they are now poised to induce major structural changes in national building markets and building materials markets.

The second version is the **informal sector**. In rural areas of the developing world it is quite common for a single (extended) family to supply the owner and the whole building team – designers and constructors. Their building work may be synchronized with agricultural work and draws largely on vernacular designs and local materials. In effect, this involves professional part-time activity. Increasingly it also refers to the builders of squatter settlements in the burgeoning cities of the developing world. Such people display a high level of skill, building for themselves or helping neighbours. This may not be their main wage-earning activity.

The third version is the **do-it-yourself (DIY) sector**, comprising amateur part-time workers. They work entirely for themselves, to provide greater comfort, to improve the market value of their property, etc., although the work does not necessarily have to be done by them. What is notable is that these people purchase their own building materials, hire or own specialized tools, and even obtain design guidance from merchants or other direct contacts with the materials and components suppliers. This market has developed in many countries in a distinct manner, has its own technical literature and its own areas of technological development. It has effectively by-passed the entire professional building industry and represents a crucial direct link between building owners and the building materials industries.

Part of the difference between these three versions of the building industry is in their respective relationships to the building materials/components industries and other sources of materials for construction. It is plain that the building materials industries will assume an even more dominant role in the future building industry, as new ideas in manufacturing come to influence both of them.

Management and the industry

To take the argument a bit further, these three types of building industry can be divided into sub-markets, markets which are not strongly linked by client organization, contracting operations, or principle resources in competition. For instance, in many industrialized countries, the private house-building industry is quite distinct from the commercial office development industry, even though both may respond similarly to significant changes in the overall condition of the national economy.

The implications of, first, identifying a multitude of building industries and, secondly, drawing analogies with completely different industries are important, for instance, in terms of: what type of client is involved? What kind of management is necessary? What do we mean by the 'project'? How will innovation occur and be disseminated? And today: what do we mean by 'quality control'?

The types of client are considered elsewhere in this study, as is 'the project'. Models of innovation and their relationship to concepts of technology are developed later.

The question of **quality assurance** (QA) has attracted much attention in recent years, being a transfer from manufacturing, notably defence industry procurement. The difficulty for the building industry arises from the central idea of QA, namely that quality is best achieved first time, defects-free, by the person actually doing the work – by careful preparation and consideration before the work is done, rather than by remedying faults discovered through efficient checking procedures after the event.

The professional building industry has a long tradition of craftmanship, with the worker checking as he (as it has usually been) goes along. However, with the proliferating division of labour, and the fragmentation of legal responsibility, greater reliance in many countries is now placed on testing and checking. The building industry has an extensive cascade of subcontracting, as well as significant numbers of self-employed and part-time workers. As QA procedures become bureaucratized, it may be difficult for the short-term employee to pick up the organization's working methods quickly enough.

As to management, the implication of QA is that more management is done by the worker him/herself. The rise of 'management education' has greatly enriched all parts of industry and commerce. The building industries plainly have greater and greater need as they fragment into more and more smaller firms – if there are 200,000 building firms in the UK, we need *at least* 200,000

Figure 10 Italian seaside agriculture (1). Ploughing the beaches in Spring.

Figure 11 Italian seaside agriculture (2). Harvesting the beaches in Summer. Photo © Foto-Offica.

managers . . . skilled in dealing with these industries, with their development.

However, I dispute the simplistic view that there is a generalized management skill, derived from some objective 'management science', unrelated to the person's technical knowledge or skill, equally transferrable to any organization, market or industry. In such cases, management is that part of common sense which cannot be applied.

It is only when we adequately define what are the various industries involved in the building industries, and what are the associated ways of organizing their work, that we will encourage the re-generation – redefinition? – of building management. The nature and structure of those industries is intimately related to their products. This chapter has drawn some exotic parallels to try to illuminate the problem (Figs 10 and 11). It seems plain that the next phases of our various building industries will involve new forms of economic, organizational and technical linkages between the building materials sectors and the building assembly sectors. Perhaps we should seek selective technology transfer between these industries within the industry, by examining what each now means by 'function'? And how they propose to interpret 'performance' or the service and shelter offered by the building?

Further reading

Basalla, G. (1988) *The Evolution of Technology*, Cambridge University Press, Cambridge.

Bemis, A.F. (1934–6) *The Evolving House* (3 vols), MIT Press, Cambridge, Mass.

Blundell-Jones, P. (1986) Beyond the black box. *Architectural Review*, July.

CIB Report (1982) *Working with the Performance Approach in Building*, Publication 64, International Council for Building Research Studies and Documentation, Rotterdam, January.

Clifton-Taylor, A. and Ireson, A.S. (1983) *English Stone Building*, Gollancz, London.

Davis, G. and Ventre, F.T. (eds) (1990) *Performance of Buildings and Serviceability of Facilities*, ASTM Special Technical Publication 1029, American Society for Testing and Materials, Philadelphia, Pa.

Architectural Design, **36**, 9, September 1966; Special issue on Ray and Charles Eames.

Fitzmaurice, R. (1938) *Principles of Modern Building*, HMSO, London.

Gellner, E. (1970) Concepts and society, in *Sociological Theory and Philosophical Analysis* (eds D. Emmet and A. MacIntyre), Macmillan, London.

Herbert, G. (1978) *Pioneers of Prefabrication*, Johns Hopkins University Press, Baltimore, Md.

Herbert, G. (1984) *The Dream of the Factory-made House*, MIT Press, Cambridge, Mass.

Hewett, C.A. (1980) *English Historic Carpentry*, Phillimore, London.

Hughes, T.P. (1989) *Americans Genesis: A Century of Invention and Technological Enthusiasm*, Viking Penguin, New York.

Jackson, J.B. (1980) *The Necessity for Ruins*, University of Massachusetts Press, Amherst, Mass.

Lemer, A.C. (1992) Construction research for the 21st century, *Building Research and Information*, **20**, 1, 28–34.

Morris, P.W.G. (1988) Lessons in managing major projects successfully in a European context. *Technology in Society* **10**, 77–89

Nam, C.H. and Tatum, C.B. (1988) Major characteristics of constructed products and resulting limitations of construction technology. *Construction Management and Economics*, **6**, 133–47.

Neuhart, J., Neuhart, M. and Eames, R. (1989) *Eames Design*, Harry Abrams, New York.

Oughton, F. (1979) *Grinling Gibbons and the English Woodcarving Tradition*, Sobart, London.

Russell, B. (1981) *Building Systems, Industrialisation, and Architecture*, Wiley, London.

Segal, W. (1985) Street theatre. *Architects' Journal*, 14 August.

Wachsmann, K. (1961) *The Turning Point of Building* (trans. T.E. Burton), Reinhold, New York.

Garnham Wright, J.H. (1983) *Building Control by Legislation: The UK Experience*, Wiley, Chichester.

Zevi, B. (1978) *The Modern Language of Architecture*, Van Nostrand Reinhold, New York.

CHAPTER TEN

Representation and regularity

. . . we are able to transmit and receive a vast constellation of ideas and images, not only because our tongues and vocal chords can waggle, and our eardrums can vibrate, but also because our brain possesses the ability to coordinate word function, patterned sentence structure, and syntax. The spoken word, the tool held in the hand: regardless of why and how they developed, language and technology emerge as the two indispensable, learned skills that must have preceded any attempts by our ancestors to deliberately and wilfully keep track of the flow of events in the human environment, to reckon time, to set it all down in a logical order – to make a calendar.

Anthony Aveni, 1990

. . . representations of ideas have replaced the ideas themselves . . . Humans are predisposed by biology to live in the barbarism of the deep past. Only by an effort of will and through use of our invented representations can we bring ourselves into the present and peek into the future.

Alan C. Kay, 1991

Forms of representation in architecture and building present one of the central difficulties in the adequate description of processes. Many issues in buildings arise through their spatial location, even though this may also be associated with their changes over time. The evolution of methods for representing aspects of buildings is inextricably bound up with the search for under-lying stability and regularity.

Drawing is the most powerful tool we have in the building industry for the simultaneous manipulation of many variables in space. By its very nature, there is no defined sequence for reading a drawing, no time dimension, and hence no way of making true/false statements, unless mathematical concepts are im-ported onto the page (e.g. a dimensioned grid). It is immensely powerful in the rapid definition of image or visual characteristics, in the demonstration of underlying spatial order, in showing the arrangement in space.

However, to date, for building processes and for other fluctuat-ing flows, we have not been able to combine the graphic power of various drawing conventions with the manipulative power of scientific and mathematical symbols. In a sense, we have been able to show reservoirs and channels, but not capacity and flow.

Three new developments offer great potential. The first is the repertory of 'electronic geodesy' – remote sensing, global positioning systems, image processing. This promises to revolu-tionize our ability to represent and manipulate the terrain de-scriptions, the account of the site. The second derives from some of the work in the physics of chaos, where the computer screen has become a critical tool for the investigation of mathematical ideas. The third is the evolution of computerized video and associated image processing with animation. Together, these techniques should allow an explosion of graphic representations of building phenomena, exploiting our existing skills of graphic literacy. The very conventions of representation also can affect the character of the buildings to which they subsequently give rise.

It is apparent in the work of Tufte, in the USA, and of others that we are becoming more conscious that graphic methods can be used to *analyse* information and to *discover* pattern and image, not merely to represent them once known. It is part of a larger recognition that drawing is a form of thinking, not merely a record and presentation of a thought already completed. This should be no surprise, since we are used to the idea that speech, writing, mathematical reasoning, carving and hand-crafting are all ways of thinking, not records after the event. For instance, many will recall how they need to talk to a companion 'to get their thoughts clear', to use a form of externalization in order to discover what the (unconscious?) mind has been thinking. Indeed, it could be argued that if one is *not* drawing, or speaking, or writing, or hand-crafting, certain thoughts are somehow 'unthinkable'.

These remarks point to a further possibility: that we shall increasingly use graphic methods as a formal research tool in studying the work of the building industry.

One further example is of interest, from the work of the Italian architect Carlo Scarpa. It has been reported that he was exploring a detail using an L-shaped piece of timber as part of some fitting (see Fig. 12). He assumed it would be cut from a rectangular piece. In drawing the lines to show where the cut edges would be, he encountered the familiar problem of the draughtsman: how do the lines cross? Do they overlap? Or stop at a point? Scarpa realized that the carpenter would face an analogous problem in cutting the piece of timber (although in fact it is not a complicated task for a skilled craftsman). Eventually he decided that the carpenter should drill a small hole at the intersection of the lines, so that the saw would change tone when it then hit the void and produce a clean cut with no overrun. To complete the detail, he then designed it to have a small brass disc inserted in the circular notch left behind . . . The fascination is that in Scarpa's work, so often closely linked with the work of the craftsman, it is not only that the drawing represents the built object; the *process* of drawing can sometimes represent the process of making that object.

Designers have used graphic methods in some of these ways for centuries, but without a clear acknowledgement of their power as an active tool, beyond the presentation of material for contemplation. They have used them in comprehending and identifying certain regularities in the organization of buildings and spaces. These regularities have been captured as trophies in defining the stable or invariant properties of built form. Central to this tradition of architectural composition has been the concept of 'type'.

Type

The idea of **type** is important to theories of architecture and building, related to the idea of 'archetype'. It was given clearest

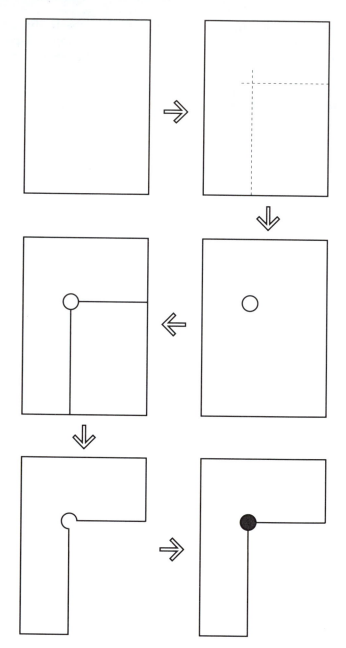

Figure 12 Sequence of developing a detail by Carlo Scarpa. The L-shaped element is developed and eventually embellished.

first formulation in the late 18th century, drawing on the work of the French theorist Laugier and his proposition of *The Primitive Hut*, which defined the fundamental characteristics of a building constructed from local natural resources.

Another French theorist of the period suggested that it be differentiated from the repetition of standard model:

> The word 'type' represents not so much the image of a thing to be copied or perfectly imitated as the idea of an element that must itself serve as the rule for the model . . . The model, understood in terms of the practical execution of art, is an object that must be repeated such as it is; type, on the contrary, is an object according to which one can conceive works that do not resemble one another at all.

We can identify two distinct ways in which 'type' may be used to describe buildings: function or use; technology.

Type by use is the driving notion from the 18th century. The American historian Anthony Vidler has shown how the approach was absorbed into the classification of natural objects which characterized 19th century science. It was a way of organizing historical data whilst seeking to keep future options free. Another French architect, Durand, devised a compositional method for architectural design in which elements were combined on gridded paper according to a comparative taxonomy of 'buildings of every *genre*'. The grid was defined by the smallest unit. Combined with the geometrical logic of mass-produced components – stamped, cast, extruded, etc. – this plainly defines a method which today we would call the 'component approach'.

Type by technology is the formulation by which we characterize buildings by the materials and constructional method – 'rationalized traditional', 'steel frame with composite cladding', etc. It is much less developed as an analytic tool, partly because we have yet to define adequately a technological paradigm in building.

More generally, Vidler has argued that since the 18th century three dominant typologies have driven the formal approach to building design. The first assimilates architecture to nature, the model of primitive shelter derived from Laugier. It reminds us of the primary function of buildings to protect us from the environment. It conjures an image of the building constructed from natural materials immediately to hand, the authenticity of the vernacular.

The second typology assimilates architecture and building to the world of machine production, with the rise of the Industrial Revolution throughout Europe and North America. This still commands the way we conceive of buildings as engineered objects with predictable performance, as machines, resulting from a highly industrialized base. It is located by Emile Zola's character Lantier, sitting on the roof of Les Halles in Paris, who remarks: 'This will kill that: iron will kill stone.'

Vidler's third typology locates itself – and takes its meanings from – the traditional city with its historic centre; it invokes concerns of context, of gradual change and 'growing old gracefully', of well-understood public spaces, of civic buildings and monuments, of transformation whilst maintaining an underlying stability – a process of equilibration, of continuous change whilst remaining at all times poised.

These three typologies thus describe three orthodox forms of stability – the building, the industry, the context. Yet all of these can be called into question.

Such approaches to the idea of type imply repetition. Yet one of the central difficulties of all attempts to learn from building experience is that we are not able to construct the 'repeatable experiment', unlike the natural sciences. In effect, we build a prototype every time. But we seek the underlying regularities of that succession of prototypes; and that has been the central puzzle for building science as it confronted building technologies.

The development of architectural composition also represents the idea of harmony, the pursuit of balance in the spatial arrangement of the parts of buildings. That very idea therefore implies a differentiation into separate elements. Once that intellectual step has been taken, it opens the door to division of labour and specialization. Fragmentation is essential to this aesthetic idea.

American author Richard Sennett takes this a step further, in emphasizing how, from the 18th century onwards, the Enlightenment ideal of 'wholeness' has passed into a modern definition of the integrity of well-made things. This concept has modified our perception of buildings from structures which extended an existing continuum of urban fabric to discrete objects, objects with an integrity which would be destroyed by change or addition. We can see the distinction from, say, Italian Renaissance

Figure 13   Church front in Urbino, Italy. Note how the construction has been adapted many times as openings and the roof line have changed. The idea that the building design must be fixed at the time of initial design has become much more forceful since the 18th century.

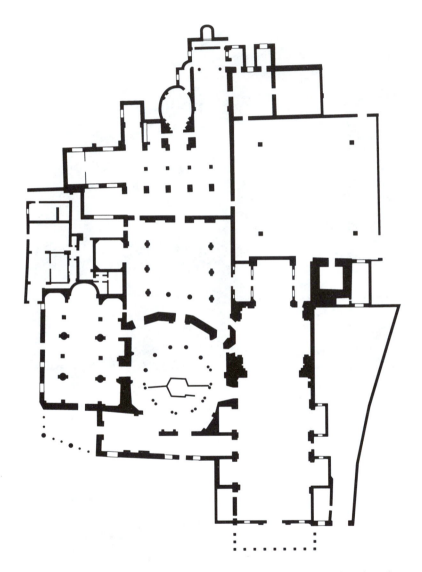

Figure 14 Plan of the Basilica of Santo Stefano, Bologna, Italy. This plan shows the overlapping of possibly seven different church spaces. It raises questions about the 'integrity' of a single building – as does the whole city of Bologna.

156

Figure 15 Piazza in San Gimignano, Italy. Note the ways in which the buildings have been continuously modified over time.

building – where many famous buildings were developed piece-meal over decades (Figs 13–16), if at all – to the modern pre-occupations with conservation, preservation and the authentic (a term used where sometimes 'unmistakable' would be more appropriate). It is but one of the later manifestations of the debate about wholes and parts.

The concepts of type and of harmony are part of the repertory of stabilities with which the makers of buildings have created traditions. Are they still helpful?

Figure 16 Piazza in San Gimignano, Italy. Note the ways in which the buildings have been continuously modified over time.

The problem of integration

The 19th century British scientist Herbert Spencer suggested that systems become increasingly differentiated and that this then redefines the integration of parts which may have experienced varying kinds of independent evolution. He regarded systems as being of greater development if they displayed extensive differentiation and integration.

It has become a truism – at least in many industrialized economies – that one of the central dilemmas of the building process is the separation of design and production, distinctive of fragmentation, represented often as the divorce of design and construction. If we acknowledge the argument above, that fragmentation is merely a property of harmony, then the complaint about divorce is a false problem. The issue is: what kind of integration is appropriate?

Idea and image

At the end of the 18th century, the German poet Friedrich von Schiller wrote an extraordinary analysis of poets. He divided them into the 'naïve' and the 'sentimental' (or 'reflective'). Subsequently, other authors extended the proposition to other forms of creative work.

The naïve poets are those who see Nature plainly, as it were looking straight out of an open window. In their writings we are not conscious of the personality of the author, the intermediary. Such authors work 'on the material itself', at the level of image.

By contrast, the sentimental poets are those who present us with an intellectual reconstruction of Nature. We are constantly aware of the author's personality; indeed, many will also write manifestos to ensure that we understand their position. Such authors work at the level of an idea, a proposition capable of verbal expression and explicit logical development.

This distinction is helpful in understanding the different approaches of building designers, such as some contemporary architects. The British architect Richard Rogers has produced designs which embody an *idea* of public space subject to change, provided in a flexible building; an example is the Lloyds' Building in London. Although this building has a distinctive appearance, its organization is not driven by an image but rather by that idea.

The Danish architect Jörn Utzon produced few complete descriptions of the Sydney Opera House, apart from some startling and enduring sketches. Yet, on inquiring of those involved in both the design and the production of this building, we discover that those images provided a continuity, a stable image, which enabled many of those people to maintain a coherence in their work.

This venture transcends conventional propositions of 'Classic vs Romantic' or 'Theoretical vs Pragmatic'. Idea or image may equally provide the generating force of a building design or of a building process. They are alternative ways of portraying stability and coherence, for buildings have always to appeal to the mind.

The task now is to discover further methods for representing – and therefore for magnifying – our thoughts about the irregularities, the instabilities, the far-from-equilibrium conditions. This will not mean discarding powerful tools and methods which have served us well. We know from the study of printing that these technologies of representation for the mass audience are infusive, pervasive agents of change.

Further reading

Aveni, A.F. (1990) *Empires of Time: Calendars, Clocks, and Cultures*, I.B. Tauris, London.

Booker, P.J. (1979) *A History of Engineering Drawing*, Northgate, London.

Boulding, K.E. (1956) *The Image*, University of Michigan Press, Ann Arbor, Mich.

Crippa, M.A. (1986) *Carlo Scarpa* (1984) (trans. S. Chapman and P. Pinna), MIT Press, Cambridge, Mass.

Eisenstein, E.L. (1979) *The Printing Press as an Agent of Change*, Cambridge University Press, New York.

Frascari, M. (1984) The tell-the-tale detail. *Via*, **7**, 22–37.

Hambly, M. (1988) *Drawing Instruments, 1580–1980*, Sotheby's, London.

Laugier, M.A. (1977) *An essay on architecture* (1753) (trans. W. and A. Herrmann), Hennessey and Ingalls, Los Angeles.

Middleton, R. (ed.) (1982) *The Beaux Arts and 19th Century French Architecture*, Thames & Hudson, London.

Panofsky, E. (1968) *Idea: A Concept in Art Theory* (1924) (trans. J. Peake), Harper and Row, New York.

Quatremère de Quincy (1977) Type. *Oppositions*, 8, Spring.

Richardson, A.E. and Corfiato, H.O. (1938) *The Art of Architecture*, Hodder and Stoughton, London.

Rossi, A. (1982) *The Architecture of the City* (trans. D. Ghirardo and J. Ockman), MIT Press, Cambridge, Mass.

Seagrim, G.N. (1967–8) Representation and communication. *Transactions of the Bartlett Society*, **6**, 11–23.

Sennett, R. (1990) *The Conscience of the Eye*, Alfred A. Knopf, New York.

von Schiller, F. (1966) *Naïve and Sentimental Poetry* (1800); *On the Sublime* (1801) (trans. J.A. Elias), Frederick Ungar, New York.

Summerson, J. (1980) *The Classical Language of Architecture*, rev. edn, Thames & Hudson, London.

D'Arcy Thomson (1961) *On Growth and Form* (1917) (abridged and ed. J. Bonner), Cambridge University Press, Cambridge.

Tufte, E.R. (1983) *The Visual Display of Quantitative Information*, Graphics Press, Cheshire, Conn.

Tufte, E.R. (1990) *Envisioning Information*, Graphics Press, Cheshire, Conn.

Vidler, A. (1978) The third typology, in *Rational Architecture: The Reconstruction of the European City*, Archives d'Architecture Moderne, Brussels.

Vidler, A. (1987) *The Writing of the Walls*, Princeton Architectural Press, Princeton, NJ.

Villari, S. (1990) *J.N.L. Durand (1760–1834): Art and Science of Architecture* (trans. E. Gottlieb), Rizzoli, New York.

Wildbur, P. (1988) *Information Graphics*, Trefoil, London.

CHAPTER ELEVEN

Technology transfer

Practical men who believe themselves to be quite exempt from any intellectual influences are usually the slaves of some defunct economist.

John Maynard Keynes

Historically, we have used six distinct but not mutually exclusive methods to transmit knowledge about ways of building, from one generation to the next. This process is now called **technology transfer**, involving:

- apprenticeship;
- peer group learning;
- simulation of practice;
- observation;
- didactic teaching and learning;
- personal or directed study of literature.

Apprenticeship

There have been various forms of apprenticeship over the ages, which involve working on the job with someone knowledgeable, observing their methods, investing in the tools of that trade, absorbing their culture, practising under their scrutiny ('learning by Nellie').

Builder Michael Hatchett has demonstrated how rich and complex has been the history of craft-based apprenticeship in the UK building industry. It involves a great deal more than the straight-forward acquisition of manual dexterity for certain tasks related to given occupations.

In Europe, the initial phase of systematic craft development in building began with merchant guilds established during the 12th century, becoming part of the web of social and administrative systems. A particularly interesting example comes from the studies by Australian historian John James. He has explored the work of itinerant medieval master masons and their 'building campaigns' for the phased construction of the Gothic cathedrals and churches in Northern France. The roles of the guilds diverged in the different European countries and, in some countries, the guilds and their apprenticeship systems remained until quite recently a powerful method of transferring know-how.

By the 14th century, in the City of London, for instance, citizen-ship and craft guild membership became linked, as the 'master craftsman' became recognized as someone with mastery of a body of established knowledge and skill. Apprenticeship was a procedure by which a person was linked to a master craftsman of such guilds, although it is unclear what commitment to training was placed at that time upon the master.

Britain experienced complex developments, partly because of the role of craft qualifications in upward social mobility. Between the 16th and 19th centuries, the concept of the seven-year appren-ticeship emerged, alongside a considerable amount of inter-guild disputes. The rise of the trade unions changed the relationships of craftsmen from then on. From the early 19th century, anyone in the UK could set up in a trade, or start a business, without having served an apprenticeship. Voluntary apprenticeship con-tinued in the building industry until the 1960s, when the UK government introduced new concepts of industrial training. In the early 1980s, Hatchett suggested that apprenticeship could be seen as a conflict between learning and earning, from the appren-tice's viewpoint, and between training and production from the employer's point of view. The adequacy of apprenticeship there-fore turns on a dilemma: the success of harmonizing the interests of training and production.

Behind the system is an assumption that, over the apprentice-ship period, the apprentice will several times encounter most of the practical situations they have to master. They will learn not only from the master, but also from their own experience – and

164

will have learnt how to continue to do so on their own. This model therefore implies a significant degree of stability in building methods.

Peer-group learning

The employment structure of the building industry is highly volatile – more so in recent years with the increase of sub-contracting. The building team is often newly constituted for each project. All participants are constantly having to establish working relationships with new people, for instance, in joint problem-solving.

In such a situation, one of the constants is the peer group of people working in the same, or similar, occupations. As a continuation of the guild tradition, peer groups may well provide technical support to their members. Individuals will also support each other and exchange ideas and methods. One of the implications of the current trend to more specialized subcontractors is that there should be much greater opportunities for peer-group learning. It remains to be seen how far the division of labour has delivered this benefit.

Simulation

The simulation of practical tasks is one of the principal methods used in schools for all the building disciplines. The benefit is that the work can be rehearsed without the costs or penalties for unacceptable work of a live contract; and it can be paced or even interrupted to allow discussion and reflection on the work at hand. It is a process which admits and can be changed by criticism.

The significant variable is the extent to which these methods seek to mimic the complete reality. In some cases, the simulation is of a simplified reality: all the elements present may occur in reality, but not all those present in practice are included in the simulation. In some, it involves a combination of simplified reality and other constraints or opportunities which might not arise, in practice, but which are seen as educationally beneficial. However, two residual questions remain: how can we be sure

165

that we have successfully mimicked today's reality? And how do we go about mimicking that of tomorrow?

Observation

Because of site-based production and the interactive functions of the building team, people involved in the building process have many opportunities to observe other occupations at work. As American sportsman Yogi Berra has pointed out: 'You can observe a lot just by watching.'

A particular form of systematic observation which has emerged in recent years is that of the 'participant-observer', borrowing techniques from anthropology. In this version, the observer has a proper role in the activity and is not there purely to observe. This method recognizes that such an observer cannot be 'neutral' or 'invisible', especially in industrial situations where those at work are aware that their output rate may be a matter of management scrutiny.

It can be argued that the documentation of modern building technology is always obsolescent because the industry changes so rapidly. The knowledge of experienced craftsmen may be similarly limited. It follows that the only place to discover and understand current methods is at the point of production – on the site or in the factory. In Japan, research is underway to develop 'point of production' observation and monitoring which will not interfere with that production. Developments of this kind will form part of what is discussed below as the role of the 'practitioner-researcher' in the building industry.

Didactic teaching and learning

Under this heading we find the familiar range of formal academic methods for transferring information, theories, work methods, etc. This includes lectures, tutorials, seminars, workshops and all the other methods which flow from a teacher-centred concept of study. There has been a much greater reliance on such methods for all the building disciplines over the last century or so, strengthened by the rise of building science, by the development of 'scientific' industrial management, and by the penetration of art history into the study of architecture and design.

Personal or directed study of literature

Textbooks of architecture and building have been available for centuries. Some of their contents were regarded as a necessary component of the education of the wealthy, whatever their occupation, and meant a common culture between some clients and some designers.

If a builder from the 15th century were to observe a building project in one of the more industrialized countries in the late 20th century, perhaps the biggest difference they would notice is the amount and types of documentation, in part developed through the greater control made possible by the new forms of representation, discussed above.

There is now an extraordinary volume and complexity of study literature in building disciplines. Along with the rise of many specialisms, we have seen the rise of the specialized technical journals. We have also experienced the evolution of manufacturers' literature – from essentially promotional functions to general descriptions to technical specification or even certification – although the transformation will never be complete.

Some of this exists for general reference, as mandatory requirements (e.g. legislation to protect the general public, building control) or associated with them (e.g. standards). Some is available as textbooks, manufacturers' literature, research reports, building case studies, building element guides, lessons from building pathology, recommendations for good practice, feedback notes, checklists and rules-of-thumb, articles in the technical press and other guidance.

Each organization involved in a given building project will have its own internal documentation – employment contracts for the staff, insurance policies, guidelines to office practice, etc.

A significant quantity is produced specifically for a project – briefs, site studies, contracts, specifications, calculations, submissions for statutory approvals, drawings, network analyses, records of resources scheduled and used, orders and receipts, correspondence, financial accounting, progress reports, etc.

Behind this explosion of information, instruction and guidance is a set of assumptions which, in effect, come from a communications model of the industry, a model which proposes a particular form of stability and of which quality assurance techniques are the latest incarnation.

Assumptions of stability

Behind these six categories of knowledge transfer are three critical assumptions of stable practice in the building industry. The first assumption is that there exists a **continuity of learning**. This means that all six forms of learning continue to operate, in roughly the patterns we have known for decades.

The second assumption is that we have a **continuity of technology**, that we retain a substantial repertory of well-tried and reliable technical precedents. These are known informally throughout the industry and are also adequately documented in textbooks, etc. They have survived the test of time, because they have proved to be insensitive to errors of design, manufacture, assembly or use.

The third assumption is that there is a **continuity of theory and practice**. That is, because building theories have been derived from the study of practice, there always exists a suitable practical example and application of the theoretical ideas, often expressed in 'typical details'.

All three assumptions have to be questioned.

The continuity of learning has been disrupted by doubts about both apprenticeship methods and didactic structures. In some countries this has developed as part of a complex programme in which it is proposed that industrial training should be primarily the responsibility of the industry concerned. In the case of the building industry, with a significant proportion of the workforce either self-employed or working for specialist subcontractors, this strategy presents major problems.

The continuity of technology is fractured by difficulties with achieving satisfactory performance in well-established methods of construction and servicing of buildings.

The continuity of theory and practice has in fact presented many problems in formal education for some time. This has usually been presented as a matter of the technical competence of those learning – e.g. as with the sympathetic comment on architecture students by UK architect Martin Kenchington in 1952:

Technical lectures are by contrast regarded as drudgery; the materials and processes described are seldom seen and more seldom performed, although some schools organise site visits . . . Rival critics have pushed more and more subjects into the syllabus, which despite repetition are not quite grasped for lack of time and which consequently create the pathetic lack of confidence of young architects . . .

All three assumptions rest on a further issue: what kind of knowledge is involved in the making of buildings? And is the critical issue in technology transfer that of transmitting information?

There is reason to believe that the most critical factor may be the interest of the recipient of building knowledge. Young people in the building disciplines often wonder why they have to rehearse technical methods immediately, rather like St Augustine's famous prayer: 'Dear God, make me chaste; but not just yet.'

Forms of building knowledge

The six categories of learning set out above run from the most 'tacit' to the most 'explicit' knowledge, where the term 'tacit knowledge' is taken from the writings of the Hungarian scientist Michael Polanyi. Tacit knowledge is that which we need for action, to do something – like riding a bicycle, but which cannot be articulated or externalized.

Tacit knowledge is also acritical – it cannot be undermined by direct criticism. In the case of bicycle riding, for instance, we cannot teach someone to ride by simply getting them to learn off by heart a series of instructions; they have to learn also by practice. Conversely, we cannot undo their ability by criticizing the principles of balance.

Explicit knowledge is that which can be communicated to other people in speech, writing, drawings, scientific notation, etc. It includes formal arguments and theories. However, merely knowing it is not sufficient for action. We have to learn also to operationalize that explicit knowledge. But the explicit element of that knowledge can be cast into doubt by formal criticism – e.g. the empirical refutation of a scientific theory, or the disproof of a previously accepted mathematical theorem.

The central task for building education has always been to combine these two forms of knowledge as each has developed, partly together, partly separately.

These forms are sometimes represented in physical objects

which are part of the processes of building. These are tools and machines, which exist as reified knowledge. Tools, of course, are also designed with the ergonomics of their operators in mind, especially how they may be held and manipulated in space to exercise force or other control.

A final consideration relates to a crucial distinction of transmission practices as between science and technology. As American historian Elizabeth Eisenstein has demonstrated, the printing press made scientific ideas and developments available internationally, far more rapidly than word of mouth or personal contact. The principle of documentation was significant in the rise of science. By contrast, those engaged in making things, in technologies, have usually been 'papyrophobic', reluctant to commit themselves to paper, to set down their procedures and doctrines. The building industry is a good example, despite the emergence of specifications over the last century or so. The evidence of technological development is less formalized; the role and traditions of transmitting knowledge have skirted the written document. They are not part of the operating practices; in some medieval memorial, they almost seem to intrude upon the authenticity of making things.

With demands for new building skills, such as maintenance (especially in building systems), will we continue to suspect the documentation and naming, muddling to renew the myth of Rumpelstiltskin?

Further reading

Ashford, J.L. (1989) *The Management of Quality in Construction*, Spon, London.

Eisenstein, E.L. (1979) *The Printing Press as an Agent of Change*, Cambridge University Press, Cambridge.

Gruber, W.H. and Marquis, D.G. (eds) (1969) *Factors in the Transfer of Technology*, MIT Press, Cambridge, Mass.; see especially D. Price, Publication in science and technology.

Harvey, J. (1975) *Medieval Craftsmen*, Batsford, London.

Hatchett, M. (1982) An investigation into the relevance and cost of building craft provision in two geographical areas of England, unpublished M.Phil thesis, Council of National Academic Awards, Polytechnic of Central London, February 1982.

Innocent, C.F. (1971) *The Development of English Building Construction* (1916), David & Charles, Newton Abbot.

Landes, D.S. (1969) *The Unbound Prometheus*, Cambridge University Press, Cambridge.

Laudan, R. (ed.) (1984) *The Nature of Technological Knowledge: Are Models of Scientific Change Relevant?*, D. Reidel, Dordrecht.

Polanyi, M. (1958) *Personal Knowledge*, Routledge and Kegan Paul, London.

Wittkower, R. (1952) *Architectural Principles in the Age of Humanism*, 2nd edn, Tiranti, London.

CHAPTER TWELVE

Who is the builder?

The people involved in assembling buildings on sites in different countries have organized themselves and their work in an extraordinary variety of ways, but only recently have we seen the *simultaneous* variety – bewildering in its volatility.

We are considering an industry which, world-wide, accounts for around US $1000 billion worth of work each year, aside of the largely unrecorded volume of self-help housing in poor countries with large populations. (The UK volume is around US $60 billion, France at around US $80 billion.) It adds probably 3–5% by value each year to the existing stock of buildings and works. It employs perhaps 50 million people and, on average, provides 6.5% of Gross Domestic Product (GDP). (In Europe, this is more like 8%, even 10% in the EC.)

Will it need the same spectrum of technical, organizational and managerial skills in the future? How can we tell? Who will build?

In his seminal book, *The Building of Renaissance Florence*, American historian Richard Goldthwaite argues that despite various reorganizations of the building process since Ancient Greece and Rome (temple-building comprised only a small market sector), European and American building industries have changed only slowly, if at all, until the Industrial Revolution. He himself has demonstrated how the 15th century Florentine building industry made extensive use of subcontracting – it is not a 'modern disease'! Studies of British royal construction programmes show the constant use of forced labour, policed to prevent desertion, well into the 14th century. Contracting for specific trades dates from that period.

Later, with urbanization and industrialization in Europe changing the scale and concentration of building activities, new forms of building organization emerged, notably the general builder (a single organization encompassing all the principal building trades). The linking of the building industry (as we might begin to define it) with the processes of land development induced a major distinction in building production systems: we find the contrast between speculative building, where the builder is the developer and source of finance, and general contracting, where the general builder makes a contract with a distinct client/owner or developer to produce a building to their specification.

In the past thirty years, we have seen a vast flourishing of mutations and hybrids, as market circumstances, employment conditions, shifts of work from building site to factory, new plant and equipment, sources of finance, forms of accountability, technological change and forms of contract have churned and brought to the surface ever-evolving ways of arranging the building process. The most distinct change has been in the nature of the skills needed to organize such work. In the words of English engineer Derek Sugden: 'We used to work in the building trade; today, we work in the construction industry.'

What forms of management are appropriate to the organization of building work in the immediate future? How do we confront the manifest evolution – if not revolution – in the building industries of wealthy countries where we find so many changes:

- Trends to greater specialization;
- Decline in reliable technical precedents;
- Greater intervention in the building process by clients/owners;
- A more dominant role for the building materials industries (manufacturing) as the source of formal R & D, in future likely to be informed by scientific research in a fashion hitherto unknown;
- More work to existing buildings (in the UK, this now accounts for more than 50% of the work by value, if we acknowledge DIY and the 'black economy');
- New uses for buildings which, in turn, are rapidly varied (what Americans call 'the churn');
- New ways of using and controlling space in buildings over time.

- An explosion of control methods in environmental and other services, just as we discover doubts about their fundamental suitability;
- Further fragmentation of the industry, paralleled by new forms of the developer role – their emergence as potential consultants for large public and private organizations moving from a 'provider' role to a 'procurer' role in relation to the building industry;
- Concepts of facilities management and the total provision of building services;
- The emergence of quality assurance and other 'process re-liability' systems, founded in the doctrine that rational control of the process will ensure a satisfactory product;
- The likely dominance of concepts of 'consumer protection' replacing the previous doctrine of 'let the buyer beware';
- The growth of litigation and the implications for professional indemnity, insurance, warranties, etc;
- Changing concepts of what constitutes building research and development;
- Changing relationships between the use of time and money and their meanings for design and function.

What skills and experience will be relevant for designers, constructors, craftsmen and women, and others engaged in the building processes of the future? Will we share the vision of American analyst Rosabeth Moss Kanter that future professional/ managerial classes will cease to enjoy a career in the traditional sense? That their development will be personal rather than corporate? That they will need to know how to share skills and knowledge, to combine rapidly with new people for discrete projects? Or are these precisely the skills that managers of work throughout the building process – their own or other people's – have always displayed?

If this is the case, how far is it necessary to retain that skill in the organization of space or time, or both, despite the improved abilities we now have to manipulate and evaluate the value of money – its flows and reservoirs – throughout the process? Are those socio-technical skills learnt only through knowledge and experience of the technologies of building, through the processes of making? This is not to complain about the introduction of financial and management skills in the building industry, many of which are long overdue, but one has to ask: what are their consequences for the future organization and quality of building work? Or should we insist that building management must start with a knowledge of building?

Further reading

Ball, M. (1988) *Rebuilding Construction*, Routledge, London.

Braithwaite, D. (1981) *Building in the Blood*, Godfrey Cave, London.

Colvin, H.M. (1963–76) *The History of the King's Works*, vols 1–5, HMSO, London.

Edmonds, G.A. and Miles, D.W.J. (1984) *Foundations for Change: Aspects of the Construction Industry in Developing Countries*, Intermediate Technology Publications, London.

Goldthwaite, R.A. (1980) *The Building of Renaissance Florence*, Johns Hopkins University Press, Baltimore, Md.

Harris, F. and McCaffer, R. (1989) *Modern Construction Management*, 3rd edn, Blackwell Scientific Publications, London.

Hobhouse, H. (1971) *Thomas Cubitt – Master Builder*, Macmillan, London.

Kanter, R.M. (1989) *When Giants Learn to Dance*, Simon & Schuster, New York.

Postgate, R.W. (1923) *The Builders' History*, National Federation of Building Trade Operatives, London.

Strassmann, W.P. and Wells, J. (eds) (1988) *The Global Construction Industry*, Unwin Hyman, London.

CHAPTER THIRTEEN

The idea of technology, and its critics

Much of the text in Book Two has concentrated on the ways in which science and technology have transformed buildings and building processes. I have sought to qualify these approaches, to demonstrate that not only do they have to be set in a social and industrial context, but that they do not represent unambiguous objectivity. I have also attempted to use some new concepts from science to reflect back on previous methods of building, to show that they may illuminate the successful solutions we have invented over the centuries.

This is not an attempt to show that buildings and the building industry have fundamentally failed. On the contrary, it is intended to introduce a new way of understanding why things have worked rather well on many occasions.

The emphases have been largely on what I have called the professional building industry, as practised in the industrialized countries, and on their advanced technical preoccupations, because I believe that this has dominated change in the past 200 years and has tacitly given us the language and the organizational structures which will condition the immediate future. However, perhaps we should now pay more attention to the underlying methods in the other building industries I have identified, including learning the lessons of how to build in a poor economy: only the rich countries have the *choice* of appropriate technologies.

The thrust of the argument is that we cannot continue in the future as we believe we have performed in the past. Part of the change must be with our approach to **technology** in building. Not least, because we have seen the disappearance of the design and production professions from the commanding heights of the building economies, as the vectors of the 21st century industries emerge from a world of environmental awareness, multinational industries beset by local nationalism, global information structures, volatile commercial structures.

It is however still the very idea of technology that strikes a sour note for some people. In the sharpest version, expounded in 1983 by the Canadian architect Alberto Pérez-Gómez, it is asserted that technology can never be a determinant of architecture, and that the pursuit of this aim is not only futile in its own terms, but detrimental to architecture itself.

He argues more generally on a phenomenological basis against any systematic structuring of the design process, whether through typologies or anything else. It is an attack on the use of abstraction or pathology in the practice of building, an invocation of the medieval belief that the book interposed itself between Man and true experience. The role of tradition is unclear in his formulation, but he restricts theory and scholarship to matters of interpretation and historical reconstruction.

How do we confront such issues? First of all, the concept of 'technology' and its relationship to processes of industrial change must be examined.

The processes of industrial change

There has been an argument for some time as to the primacy of technical innovation in the process of industrial change. Some maintain that new inventions have suggested new uses, such as the Walkman cassette player: the world was not bursting with two billion people clamouring for Sony to invent this machine before it hit the market. Others have countered that social demand induces technical development, that 'necessity is the mother of invention'. Is change in the building industry supply-led or demand-led? Or should we follow American historian Thomas P. Hughes in seeing technologies as systems which embody invented techniques and invented social organizations? Do we have to identify the 'determinants' of change? Or could we not accept that there might be no determinants, only a pressing variety of *agents of change* in a turbulent environment?

Can we not accept that, as historian Cyril Stanley Smith points out, many of our heavy industries are based on understandings which began in the making of objects, often for complex non-utilitarian purposes? Early jewellery is the ancestor of modern welding and the metal industry.

Most protagonists appear to believe that research and development (R & D) programmes are necessary to sustain modern industrial change. The amounts of money thought necessary vary according to the scientific dependency and market dynamic of the particular industry. It is interesting to explore how this affects the building industry – if it is indeed an 'industry' or set of 'industries' in that sense.

It is a common complaint that the building industry under-invests in its formally funded R & D programmes by at least an order of magnitude, by comparison with manufacturing industries. Whereas manufacturing on average invests 4–6% of annual turnover in R & D, many national building industries invest less than 1%, and much of that is by the building component manufacturers.

At the same time, however, the building industry has demonstrated itself to be constantly adaptable and innovative. Indeed, it has been regarded with envy by a number of high-technology industries for its ability to adapt. It has long sustained a 'shamrock' organizational structure, involving core professionals in permanent employ, an extensive – and increasingly – subcontracted fringe of specialists, and an array of part-time workers to respond to the dappled rise-and-fall of workload.

How can this combination of little R & D and effective innovation and adaptability be so? It appears to contradict the argument that R & D is a necessary condition of innovation and change, an argument that is broadly accepted here.

The informal innovation infrastructure

The answer to this question is provided by the existence of an extensive network of informal or *de facto* R & D workers, throughout the building process, particularly in advanced practices (design and production). These people are not employed as researchers, nor is their work budgeted as R & D. In practice, such people would probably be surprised if they were told their work was R & D. Because this infrastructure of *project-based* development work is informal, invisible to conventional surveys, it lacks proper documentation – as so often is the case in technologies. It is not part of the public knowledge of the industry and the usual way of access is to recruit more of those people with the relevant experience.

A good example of this activity is the development over the last two decades of very sophisticated composite cladding methods, sometimes in the context of 'high-tech' construction. The initiative is difficult to locate; no single organization has been responsible. If we asked how much had been the R & D budget, we would probably discover a small amount in one or two manufacturers. Crucial development work has been done by architects, engineers, cost consultants, manufacturers, specialist suppliers, specialist erection teams, main contractors. The result has been a major technical innovation and its successful establishment in a commercial world. In any other industry, it would be regarded as R & D, as evidence of its necessity. We cannot acknowledge this simple fact in the building industries.

The sadness is that this informal R & D cohort do not mesh with the formally funded R & D programmes. In future, each will increasingly need the other. The building industry is poised to enter an age in which science and technology are much more strongly related, with the manufacturing base and international procurement taking over as the engines of its evolution.

Technology transfer is via peer groups, and those institutions are crumbling. As the assumption of control of current information increasingly permeates building litigation, the informal groups will come under excessive stress. The attempt at quality assurance will create a welcome clarification of practices, a tacit pressure to carry out the sensible practices we fondly or self-righteously proclaim. But the simultaneous pursuit of better information and greater transparency is not without its problems (as Chapter 6 suggests).

A case is presented in Book One for recognizing the decline of robust technologies. One of the implications is that all building projects will have to be treated as innovative, *whether or not those concerned intend them to be so.* This will lead to a greater need for research literacy on the part of all practitioners throughout the professional building industries – they will evolve to a role I call 'the practitioner-researcher'. However, simultaneously, methods of education and training are in disarray, especially if the decline of technical precedent becomes more pervasive. If the trend to a new set of roles and occupations emerges, the informal network will not be able to cope with the know-how demands; whilst the formal R & D activity risks developing along an increasingly irrelevant course defined by the concepts of 19th century scientific research.

Concepts of research and development

I suggest that the paradigm of R & D inherited from 19th century scientific research, via the early paradigm of engineering research, by itself is inadequate for the design and production of buildings.

What is needed now is a research paradigm, a framework of meaning and practice which derives from technology, from the process of making things, from the concept of 'know-how'. It will use design and production methods as the cutting edge. It will accept the idea of deterministic processes which are unpredictable. It will incorporate the critic as one of the participants in the building process, to help with establishing a useful meld between tacit and explicit knowledge, between information and skill. It will involve new versions of organizations, ones which are knowledge-based and skill-sharing, rather than simply skill-based.

Perhaps American researcher Andrew Lemer's idea of 'conovostruction' – innovatory construction with the user in mind – should be pursued?

Building behaviour is described above in terms of flows and reservoirs. This demonstrates that scientific ideas can usefully inform our ways of thinking about the nature of building. It does not follow that the process of research has to follow that of the natural sciences. A better model for practice is one in which the practitioner's skills and techniques are absorbed into the method of research and development, myths, cultural variabilities and all. It is only if we demand a technological paradigm which is genuinely situated in a social and industrial framework, that we will develop a responsive conflagration of the dynamic concepts of building and the stable ideas which provide us with their control.

Regarding education and training for the building disciplines, we must recognize that industrial change is rife there as well. This book has not tried to explore the implications for this realm; suffice it to say that change does not have to come from within existing industries, organizations or occupations. So far as I know, the electronic pocket calculator was not introduced by the manufacturers of slide rules.

Our concepts of change – indeed, our concepts of history – are, in turn, subject to historical evolution. In particular, they are today entwined with concepts of 'progress' and 'the future', probably derived from the work of the Enlightenment in 18th century Europe. However, we find anomalies, the tortoise and the hare. In 1926 John Logie Baird invented the first TV; in 1927 the British Army formally abandoned the lance as a weapon, except for certain ceremonial purposes . . .

Technological change has to be distinguished from progress, for which it may be a necessary but is not a sufficient condition. We believe we can predict the future, in some degree, by carrying the past with us. Perhaps we should remember that South American tribe in whose language the word for 'the front of the body' is the same as the word for 'the past', and the word for 'the back of the body' is the same as the word for 'the future'. They picture themselves walking backwards into the future, able to see the flow of what has happened, incapable of *conceiving* what is to come.

The dilemma of stability and change is neatly displayed in the frequent assertion: 'You shouldn't reinvent the wheel.' Yet we do so constantly. We know that succession as a rolling log, the splayed cartwheel, the bicycle wheel, the pneumatic tyre, the caterpillar track, the ball-bearing, the castor, the hovercraft, the banana skin. As we have redefined or changed the circumstances in which the wheel is used, we have redesigned and reproduced its essential features, including the means by which it is conceived, designed and made. There is every reason to suppose that we should treat buildings in similar fashion.

Further reading

Allen, T.J. (1977) *Merging the Flow of Technology: The Transfer and Dissemination of Technological Information within the Research and Development Organisation*, MIT Press, Cambridge, Mass.

Banham, R. (1984) *The Architecture of the Well-tempered Environment*, 2nd edn, Architectural Press, London.

Banham, R. (1986) *A Concrete Atlantis*, MIT Press, Cambridge, Mass.

Bann, S. (1990) *The Inventions of History: Essays on the Representation of the Past*, University of Manchester Press, Manchester.

Bijker, W.E., Hughes, T.P. and Pinch, T.J. (eds) (1987) *The Social Construction of*

Technological Systems, MIT Press, Cambridge, Mass; see especially T.P. Hughes, The evolution of large technological systems.

Bon, R. (1991) What do we mean by building technology? *Habitat International*, **15**, 1/2, 3–26.

Building and Civil Engineering Economic Development Committee (1985) *Strategy for Construction R & D*, National Economic Development Office, HMSO, London.

Business Roundtable (1983) *More Construction for the Money*, New York, Business Roundtable.

Cooley, M. (n.d.) *Architect or Bee?*, Langley Technical Services, Slough.

Cooper, C. and Kaplinsky, R. (1989) Technology and development in the Third Industrial Revolution. *European Journal of Development Research*, Special issue, **1**(1), June.

Dosi, G. (1982) Technological paradigms and technological trajectories. *Research Policy*, 11, 147–62.

Drewer, S. (1982) *The Transfer of Construction Techniques to Developing Countries*, LCHS Publication No. 2, University of Lund, Sweden.

Dunster, D. (1977) Critique: *Architecture and Utopia. Architectural Design*, **47**(3), 204–12.

Dunster, D. (1990) Collaborating in education: the Diploma Project at the Bartlett School, 1988–89. *Journal for Architectural Education*, **43**(2), Winter, 14–21.

Groák, S. and Krimgold, F. (1989) The practitioner-researcher in the building industry. *Building Research and Practice*, **17**(1), 52–9.

Gutman, R. (1988) *Architectural Practice: A Critical View*, Princeton Architectural Press, Princeton, NJ.

Handy, C. (1989) *The Age of Unreason*, Business Books, London.

Horwitch, M. (ed.) (1988) Macro-engineering: the new challenge, *Technology in Society*, Special issue, **10**(1).

Hughes, T.P. (1989) *American Genesis: A Century of Invention and Technological Enthusiasm*, Viking Penguin, New York.

Kanter, R.M. (1989) *When Giants Learn to Dance*, Simon & Schuster, London.

Lemer, A.C. (1992) Construction research for the 21st century. *Building Research and Information*, **20**, 1, 28–34.

Lubetkin, B. (1982) Royal Gold Medal address. *Transactions*, **1**(2), RIBA, London.

Mackenzie, D. and Wajcman, J. (eds) (1985) *The Social Shaping of Technology*, Open University Press, Milton Keynes.

Medina, M. and Sanmartin, J. (1989) A new role for philosophy and technology studies in Spain. *Technology in Society*, **11**, 447–55.

Pacey, A. (1974) *The Maze of Ingenuity: Ideas and Idealism in the Development of Technology*, Allen Lane, London.

Pawley, M. (1987) Technology transfer. *Architectural Review*, **CLXXXII** (1087), September, 31–9.

Pérez-Gómez, A. (1983) *Architecture and the Crisis of Modern Science*, MIT Press, Cambridge, Mass.

Roller, D.H.D. (ed.) (1971) *Perspectives in the History of Science and Technology*, University of Oklahoma Press, Norman, Okla; see especially C.S. Smith, Art, technology, and science: notes on their historical interaction.

Rosenberg, N. (1982) *Inside the Black Box: Technology and Economics*, Cambridge University Press, Cambridge.

Tolstoy, L.N. (1869) *War and Peace* (trans. R. Edmonds), Penguin, London; 1978 edn, especially the Epilogue.

Wagner, R. (1975) *The Invention of Culture*, Prentice-Hall, Englewood Cliffs, N.J.

Waterous, F.B. (1987) Future directions in engineering education: 'technology' as an integrative concept, in *Frontiers in Education Conference Proceedings* (eds L.P. Grayson and J.M. Biedenbach), Rose-Hulman Institute of Technology, Institute of Electrical and Electronic Engineers, USA.

BOOK THREE

Another Critical Position

Book Three attempts to develop the ideas from Books One and Two into a critical method. The figures presented here are chosen, first, because they do not sit comfortably in simple categories of architect, builder, etc. In many respects, their work represents the deliberate explorations and invocations of stable forms, invariant properties, regularities over time. Yet some also pose questions about the pervasive effects of concepts of flux. I also hope that by examining their work, or, rather, that of the organizations within which they flourished, the benefits of the earlier propositions will be apparent.

The particular focus is on: the placing and use of reservoirs in the built and organized volumes of the project; their significance for form, space and comfort; their roles in conformal mapping or the literalizing of the metaphor which so often precipitates design into production.

CHAPTER ONE

The typical detail

The notion of the 'typical detail' has rambled through building books for centuries. It depicts a joint or junction in the construction which, in some measure, stands for a complete system of building. As a graphic summary – image? – it has been one of the traditional torches of construction education and training, igniting the structure of texts and the memorable method.

The typical detail is often published without a historical reference, as if it stands for all time. Today we should ask the question: what is the history of such details? What do they tell us about the evolution of design, craft skill and building method?

Construction method

There are many strategies and pragmatic approaches for defining construction design and method. Some arise from systems of principles, and some through the established practice of a design or building organization. What emerges, however, is that when construction design can be founded in the production process of building, we have a clear basis for some of the critical decisions.

Much has been made in recent years of the benefits of **buildability**, or **constructability**. In its most useful formulation, this means that design should take proper account of how the building will be made on site. For best effect, this means knowing at the design stage which production organization will make the building since there is no single best method of making buildings, except by reference to the resources to be used.

Certain consequences flow from this position. First, it can be argued, the most important quality of construction detail is that it can be easily inspected by eye on site. Secondly, for some technologies, we may prefer to specify a lower performance standard which has a higher chance of being constructed correctly. There is a sort of 'uncertainty principle' in which the 'product' of the standard multiplied by the chance of success has a maximum: too high a performance requirement may be unreliable and it is the overall reliability which we may seek.

Other guidance arises from the nature of the material and energy flows of buildings. The problems of detailing arise whenever there is a change of geometry and/or material (and hence energy flow). These details constitute the definition of boundaries and valves to distinct reservoirs in the building – some desirable (e.g. thermal capacity within insulation), some not so desirable (e.g. valley gutters). They are discontinuities in the building, necessary sometimes to even out erratic flows, but which inevitably provide for concentrations of stress (e.g. under earthquake loading) or other matter/energy potentials. In effect, they are unwanted reservoirs along the flow lines of matter and energy, easily ruptured.

A further concern is the inherent properties of built forms and the ease of subsequent building operations, whether for repairs ('maintainability') or change of use.

Where possible, the built form should control the environmental variables and flows before they impact on the interior. The control of solar radiation is a good example.

Buildings which grow and change have some elements which are adaptable (capable of changing use) and some which are flexible (capable of changing position). Invariably there are some inflexible elements: to provide for change we have to build in spare capacity since they are very difficult to reconstruct.

Examples include the principal structure, the drainage systems, the zones for mechanical/electrical services, the floor-loading capacity, and the provision and organization of space. The implication is that these inflexible elements – which are often clearly defined reservoirs – should be built to the higher performance levels (capacity) where possible.

The provision of space is of particular interest, since some argue that we should provide maximum space, keeping finishes to a lower standard since these are more easily upgraded later on.

It is apparent that strategic approaches to construction can also be devised from an understanding of flows, without unreasonably restricting the designer or the builder.

Further reading

Architects' Journal (1988) Special issue on Walter Segal, 4 May.
Dunster, D. (1984) Mies van der Rohe and the craft of architecture. *UIA International Architect*, UIA Issue 3.
Martin, B. (1977) *Joints in Buildings*, George Godwin, London.

CHAPTER TWO

Building details in structure and form

This chapter discusses particular projects and built examples: timber-frame houses built anonymously in 14th century England, masonry structures designed by the 15th century Italian architect-builder Filippo Brunelleschi, metal-frame buildings designed by the 20th century German-American architect, Ludwig Mies van der Rohe, and the Sydney Opera House.

A language of structure

The British researcher Richard Harris, working at the Weald and Downland Museum, near Chichester, has established a convincing thesis about the way in which traditional timber-frame houses were organized. He argues that the orientation of the structure, the disposition of the pieces of timber and the character of the details are all imbued with a social significance which was well understood by the builders and by those using the buildings.

The medieval process of making and finishing the timber frame involved laying it on the ground, prior to erection. The top face was therefore available for much better treatment and had the 'fair' face of the two sides. Harris shows that the frame was invariably erected such that the fair face was presented to the socially more significant space in the house – e.g. the main room. He argues that this symbolic orientation comes from and is reinforced by the craftsman's understanding of the social order.

In a number of instances, repeated elements of a timber frame are cut from one piece of timber – e.g. cross-ties at the corners of the building. What is interesting here is that we often find that the four pieces are arranged around the structure in the spatial pattern they once had in the tree. They have been 'exploded' but have retained their natural relationship.

Harris also demonstrates that the detailed construction of frame joints is peculiar to distinct regions of the country; and all are quite different from their 14th century contemporaries in continental Europe, in Germany, Denmark, etc. He suggests that this variation is akin to the dialects and languages of different social groups.

The expression of structure

Amongst the many things to be learnt from classical Greek buildings is the way in which the support function of structure is made very plain. The principle of post-and-beam dominates the appearance of classical temples. Roof loads are collected on beams and thereby transferred down the columns to the ground. Self-weight is the dominant structural problem (compare tall structures, such as the Eiffel Tower, where lateral wind loads are the principal problem).

There has been some speculation that the slight bulge at the middle of the columns – **entasis** – and their dispositions in space are arranged to give the visual impression of the whole structure flexing under load. What is more certain is that the surface decoration effectively camouflages the assembly process. The columns are constructed by placing masonry segments one on top of another. The vertical fluting disguises the horizontal joints and presents the column as a single homogeneous element (Fig. 17). The static is preferred to the dynamic, the permanent to the temporary.

There has been a long tradition in European architecture that engineers and architects are also builders. Modern examples include the Italian engineer Pier Luigi Nervi, and the Spanish-Mexican engineer Felix Candela: in each case, working as building contractors, they have used their design skills to develop novel forms of construction, where the assembly process is implicit in the design, to win competitive tenders. Perhaps the most extraordinary of such designer-builders was Brunelleschi.

Figure 17 Greek Temple in Paestum, Italy. Note the construction of the columns: the blocks are fluted, which camouflages their assembly sequence of one block placed upon another.

Brunelleschi

Brunelleschi was innovative in all aspects of design and construction. More than most, he recognized that the form of the building and the process of its assembly were inextricably interwoven. He demonstrated the mathematical basis of visual perspective, a crucial aspect of the Renaissance preoccupation with the relationship between mathematics and the physical world, gained indirectly from the Ancient Greeks. He controlled the building site, for which he developed many inventions, such as sophisticated lifting devices.

In a succession of astonishing buildings, he identified a set of fundamental problems of composition and construction, in effect defined by the clarity of his solutions. He explored the formal relationship between wall, column, vault and dome, drawing on his studies of ancient Roman buildings.

His masterwork, the dome of Florence Cathedral, built on walls constructed a century earlier, combined the understandings of the

Gothic and Renaissance mentalities. It was particularly notable for its construction without the use of centring – the temporary construction usually used to support the structure directly from below whilst work is in progress.

In the Old Baptistry and Pazzi Chapel (Fig. 18), built in Florence during the 1420s, Brunelleschi introduced an additional 'virtual structure', using a distinct stone (*pietra serena*) to mark a

Figure 18   The Pazzi Chapel, Florence, Italy. Note how the pilasters change size according to their placement in relation to the grid of the wall planes.

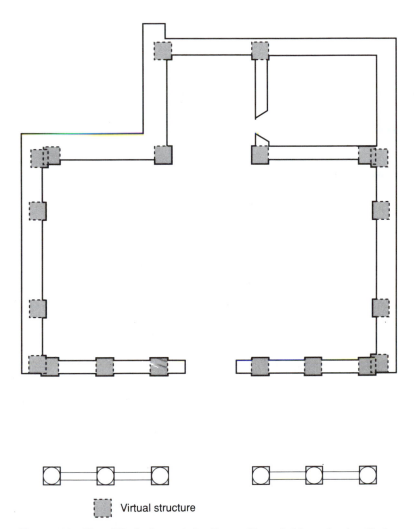

Virtual structure

Figure 19 Simplified plan of the Pazzi Chapel. Note the implied or virtual structure of 'columns', pilasters, which in fact are simply articulations of the continuous walls.

three-dimensional mathematical system in the space of the building and on the true structure. This system was defined by pure geometric forms (cubes, spheres, etc.) and by planning zones.

The detail of the *pietra serena* pilasters articulated the compositional/constructional problem of walls meeting a grid of columns. In fact, the *pietra serena* was used as a surface treatment. It defines a virtual structure (Fig. 19); the true structure is probably a continuous load-bearing wall. But the central doctrine displays a genuine design and construction problem: how are we to organize this system in space, so that frame and infill will demonstrate a consistent system, one which is buildable in the sense that we can use standard jointing, panel sizes, and so on? The rigour of Brunelleschi's concern emerged 500 years later, with the jump to recognition of steel-framed, high-rise buildings.

Mies van der Rohe

When we examine the designs of Mies, we find similar preoccupations with the spatial junction of wall and column, except that in his case these are the frame structures and window-wall cladding of the 20th century. He can be shown to have examined the problems in an extraordinarily systematic fashion. One way of classifying his designs is according to the compositional problems they confront, as expressed in Fig. 20. His building designs have set a standard for urban commercial buildings around the world since the 1950s, almost defining a new vernacular.

The special interest here is in the attitude to construction detail in Mies' work, expressed in his aphorism: 'God is in the details.' It is most apparent in the junctions between external enclosure and the primary structure. He develops themes about the expression of structure in buildings which hark back to the early Italian Renaissance and even to Ancient Greece.

Compositionally, designers are often preoccupied with how the front of a building is organized, how its 'frontality' is expressed. Where the building is intended to be approachable (in a formal sense) from different sides, there may be a deliberate attempt to signify some sort of 'equality' of different façades. If we examine the corner detail of structure and enclosure in 860–880 Lake Shore Drive, we find a symmetry about the 45° axis

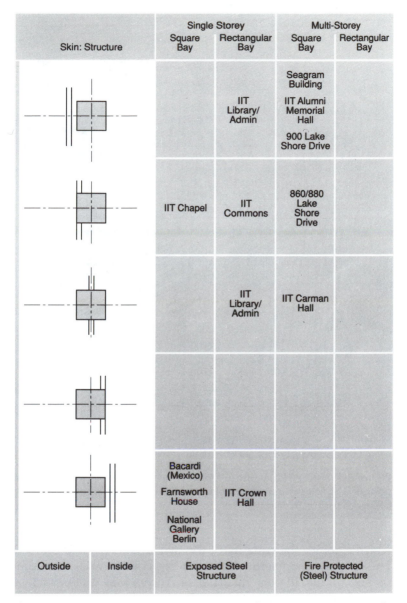

Skin: Structure		Single Storey		Multi-Storey	
		Square Bay	Rectangular Bay	Square Bay	Rectangular Bay
			IIT Library/ Admin	Seagram Building IIT Alumni Memorial Hall 900 Lake Shore Drive	
		IIT Chapel	IIT Commons	860/880 Lake Shore Drive	
			IIT Library/ Admin	IIT Carman Hall	
		Bacardi (Mexico) Farnsworth House National Gallery Berlin	IIT Crown Hall		
Outside	Inside	Exposed Steel Structure		Fire Protected (Steel) Structure	

Figure 20 Matrix to show how the designs of Mies van der Rohe can be analysed into a systematic exploration of various compositional conditions – the relation of main structure to enclosure, the explosure of the main structure, the bay shape, the height, etc. Only a sample selection of his building designs are included here.

197

Figure 21 860–880 Lake Shore Drive, Chicago, USA: apartment blocks designed by Mies van der Rohe. Hedrick-Blessing photograph, courtesy Chicago Historical Society.

which signifies the equality of the two façades (Figs 21 and 22). This occurs in many other buildings designed by Mies, including several at the Illinois Institute of Technology (IIT), such as the Alumni Memorial Hall (Fig. 23).

We also find that the structure and enclosure framing are designed as an assembly of standard hot-rolled steel sections, welded into forms which plainly derive from those of Brunelleschi and his successors. In other buildings he explores the principles

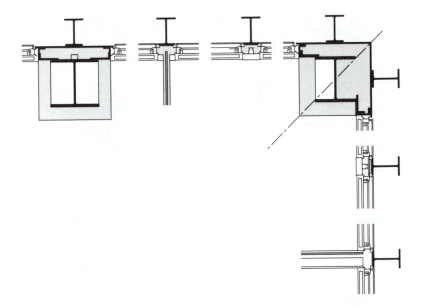

Figure 22 Detail of 860–880 Lake Shore Drive apartment blocks. Note the plan symmetry around the 45° line through the corner.

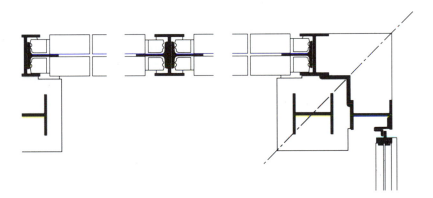

Figure 23 Alumni Memorial Hall, Illinois Institute of Technology Chicago, USA: educational building designed as part of complete campus by Mies van der Rohe. Note the plan symmetry around the 45° line through the corner and how the standard hot-rolled steel sections have been combined in the composition.

Figure 24 Farnsworth House, Illinois, USA: private house designed by Mies van der Rohe. Hedrick-Blessing photograph, courtesy Chicago Historical Society.

in a succession of materials (e.g. reinforced concrete, aluminium, bronze).

A further compositional problem had to be solved. In addition to the expression of the relationship of structure and enclosure and the frontality or equality of the façades, he sought also to

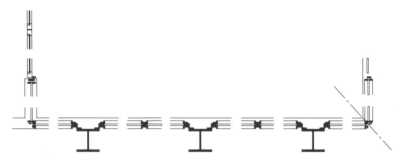

Figure 25 Plan detail of the Farnsworth House.

Figure 26 Unbuilt project for the Library/Administration Building, Illinois Institute of Technology, USA: designed by Mies van der Rohe. Note the frontality, compared with the side elevation, and the different depth of expressed roof structure (beams), because of the different spans in the two directions for a rectangular bay building.

express the relationship between load-bearing form and the supported planes of structure (floors, roof). He tried to unite two solutions: the thin plane of constant thickness and the beam structure which varied if the grid was rectangular rather than square (beam loads vary accordingly).

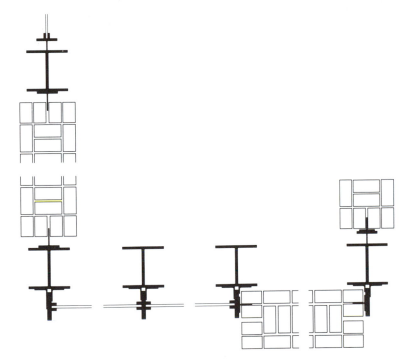

Figure 27 Plan detail of the Library/Administrative Building. Note the lack of symmetry at the corner around the 45° line, showing in detail the contrast of side and front manifest in the elevation above.

Figure 28   General view of the corner detail of the Library/Administative
Building. Mies van der Rohe, Ludwig; *Library and Administration
Building, Illinois Institute of Technology*; 1944. Corner study (southeast
corner); pencil on paper, 40 × 30″ (101.6 × 76.2 cm); Collection, Mies van
der Rohe Archive, The Museum of Modern Art, New York. Gift of the
architect.

He explored two distinct methods. The first was to place the roof
plane above the structure. If the structure was on a square grid,
he obtained a uniform horizontal plane, as in the Farnsworth
House (Figs 24 and 25). If there was a rectangular grid, he had to

Figure 29   Crown Hall, Illinois Institute of Technology, USA: architecture school on campus designed by Mies van der Rohe. Hedrick-Blessing photograph, courtesy Chicago Historical Society.

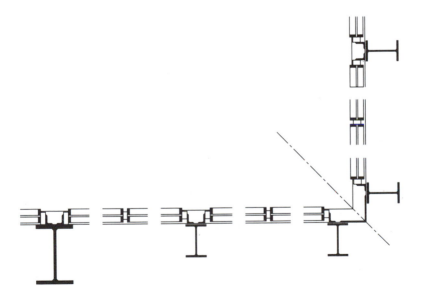

Figure 30   Plan detail of Crown Hall. Note the plan symmetry around the 45° line at the corner.

accept the change of structural banding around the building, especially where there was frontality. This is plain in the Library/ Administration project (Figs 26–28). The second approach was to use an exo-skeletal structure, with the main beams above the roof plane. This is shown in Crown Hall (Figs 29 and 30). In all cases, the organization of the detail coheres with the organization or composition of the whole building.

It has been said that Mies simplified the design problem to deal with matters he considered critical, and then solved them completely. It is clear that he concentrated on 'static' elements and excluded from serious considerations matters such as energy flows; for instance, his designs are markedly inefficient in energy terms, a product of their era.

The Sydney Opera House

The Opera House is notable for many reasons, but here I wish to concentrate on its construction on site (Fig. 31).

As Fig. 31 indicates, the main structure and enclosure of the Opera House is a series of post-tensioned precast concrete arches, tied together. They do not form a true shell structure.

One of the potent innovations was by the main contractor, in solving the problem of how to place the precast components accurately in space. In the event, they designed and constructed adjustable temporary works: a steel arch, a virtual structure, which acted as the support to one side of the impending arch as the successive segments were placed in position. The steel arch could rotate on its bearing and simply precessed through the implied geometry of the building. It was an elegant re-invention of the building's form.

Two points can be made. First, it demonstrates again that temporary works and virtual structures – the province of the contractor – can be as complex to design and construct as the permanent building; and during those stages the building components may experience their most extreme conditions.

Secondly, it highlights the difference between precision and accuracy, a practical matter which can best be illustrated with an anecdote about a visitor to a local natural history museum. The visitor, who was strolling through the exhibit rooms, chanced upon the central space, in which she found a splendid

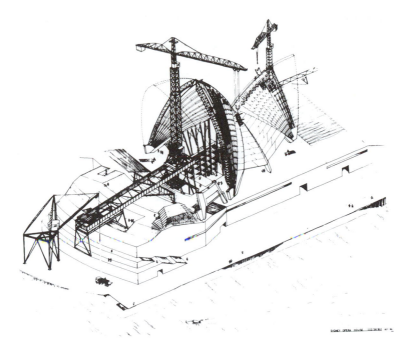

Figure 31 Sydney Opera House, designed by Jörn Utzon with Ove Arup & Partners. The drawing shows the special temporary works used in assembling the precast, post-tensioned concrete structure. The steel lattice arch rotates on a large ball at its footings, creating a temporary support for the segments of the permanent structure to be built up to a stable arch form; when the concrete arch is stable, the steel arch rotates round and creates the support for the next concrete arch.

reconstructed skeleton of a pterodactyl. Standing there admiring it, she was joined by one of the curators. She asked how old was the skeleton, to be told: 'That pterodactyl is one hundred million and seventeen years old.' Astonished, she asked how its age could be known so precisely: 'That's easy. Seventeen years ago, an archaeologist estimated that it was one hundred million years old.'

Further reading

Battisti, E. (1981) *Brunelleschi: The Complete Work* (trans. R.E. Wolf), Thames & Hudson, London.

Harris, R. (1979) *Discovering Timber-framed Buildings*, 2nd edn, Shire Publications, Princes Risborough.

Guedes, P. (ed.) (1979) *The Macmillan Encyclopedia of Architecture and Technological Change*, Macmillan, London.

Mies van der Rohe: Mansion House Square and the Tower Type, Special Issue, *UIA International Architect*, UIA Issue 3, 1984.

Renzo Piano: building workshop, 1964–88, *Architecture + Urbanism*, March 1989 (special issue)

Prager, F.D. and Scaglia, G. (1970) *Brunelleschi: Studies of His Technology and Inventions*, MIT Press, Cambridge, Mass.

CHAPTER THREE

The buildings of Alvar Aalto

This chapter explores the architectural work of the Finnish architect, Alvar Aalto (1898–1976). In the work of his office (and, of course, the work is the product of many people over 55 years) we find an astonishing synthesis of ideas about building, expressing many of the themes discussed in other chapters.

Here I attempt to introduce the relationships between the various scales of Aalto's work, which stem from his perceptions of the Finnish condition, and propose some interpretations of the actual buildings, based upon:

- Aalto's functional analysis of the Finnish economy and the changes therein following the Finno-Soviet War. Although some of these developed only in the postwar period, the basic propositions were there from the late 1920s onwards.
- Aalto's ideas of urban design, demonstrated in many industrial-residential plans, town centres, etc., growing from a conception of modern life.
- Aalto's development of civic complexes and building types, especially in relation to his humanist interpretation of functionalism.
- Aalto's synthesis of many European building traditions, his encyclopedic coverage of architectural problems and typical conditions of the 20th century.
- Aalto's use of the building type, in order to fracture and erode its unity in favour of the priority of the site.
- Aalto's approach to his work as a continuous experiment, in which no one project is complete.

- Aalto's preoccupation with the site and with routes, with memory as part of the architectural experience.
- Aalto's interest in environmental comfort and his special interest in light – treated as representative of nature, arising from his concern with a humane – often nature-oriented – functionalism.
- Aalto's use of virtually all building materials in a Constructivist tradition, in part exploring a 'layering' of the architectural volume.
- Aalto's concern to design communities and buildings which mediate between the natural order and the rational order, between Nature and the man-made environment.

A functionalist's analysis of the economy

Before the Second World War, Finland was predominantly a wood-processing economy, with communities organized around the processing plant. After the war, the industrial geography of Finland changed, as it had to deal with reparations to the USSR and with the half-million refugees from the province of Karelia, which was ceded to the USSR as a result of the Finno-Soviet War. Much of this involved substantial southward migration.

Alvar Aalto understood spatial-social relationships in the pre-war and postwar communities, as the technologies of wood harvesting and treatment radically changed. He recognized the need to respond to rapid industrialization, but nevertheless argued in favour of maintaining smaller communities. He believed that planning could not be finite, but had to allow for growth and change, especially with emerging forms of transport infrastructure, greater population mobility and new ideas of the balance between public and private initiatives – ideas given special force today in studies for the developing world. He evolved a humane functionalism, rooted in the human being's action and experience.

Urban design

Many of Aalto's buildings were built in towns or settlements where he had earlier proposed town plans or civil or industrial groupings. He had developed a full system of regional planning, arising out of a functionalist analysis of the emerging industrial structure of Finland. His concept of planning was always manifest in built form; although he understood settlement systems, he interpreted them in terms of people, infrastructure and buildings. He was highly sensitive to Finland's rural culture, and indeed was greatly influenced by Ebenezer Howard's ideas in Britain for the Garden City. Much of Aalto's planning had an urbanistic core.

His ideas were dynamic, allowing for differential growth and recognizing the different activities which had to evolve at all times providing the range of amenities and supports for a full life for the inhabitants – traffic, social issues, housing, industrial and other workplaces, aesthetic and commercial issues, and so on. Moreover, these different functions had always to be in 'dialogue'.

At the level of the town centre, his concepts allowed for the emergence of the 'citizen's square', the civic centre which acknowledged the variety of administrative, cultural, educational and social needs of the community. One of his enduring contributions to Finnish architecture has been the many civic complexes in towns around the country.

Interestingly, although he built several versions – of which that in Seinäjoki is the most fully realized – each is not only distinct as an ensemble, but there is great variety of architectural style between the buildings. He never sought, for instance, the visual coherence of the 'city beautiful' tradition.

We find similar principles at work in his rich seam of industrial/ housing developments, associated with Finland's paper industry. These mixtures form one of the principal components of his enormous output and, in many ways, are the bedrock of his particular vision of a social architecture.

Underlying all his work was an extraordinary understanding of the morphology of a site, whether for an individual building or for a larger complex. As a result, even when he could build only a fragment of an urban design, or the early phase of an industrial complex, we still find that they relate to the underlying spatial and social structure of the settlement in which they are placed. It can be argued that this structural understanding is one of the reasons why Aalto's buildings are so readily understood in their basic organization, even when their visual characteristics are apparently strange and their forms are novel.

Aalto's use of typologies

Aalto first visited the Mediterranean in 1924. He had a close attachment to the classical architecture of Italy and Greece; and Italian architects have long been admirers of his work, especially its 'organic' qualities. So it is of particular interest that an Italian historian of architecture and urbanism, Benevolo, should draw our attention to the significance of typology in Aalto's work. He writes, 'Aalto is pre-eminently a typologist'.

Aalto was wide-ranging in his use of materials and technologies of building; we cannot argue, as we are able to do with other major builders or architects, that he limited himself to a particular method or material repertory. Compositionally, although he used familiar forms when appropriate, his work is generally so distinctive in the forms it uses that, in effect, it undermines the argument that architects have to design entirely from precedent. Similarly, he has not been copied to any significant extent in his formal 'language' or style – we have only to see how Mies van der Rohe virtually defined that of the modern urban frame building to understand the strangeness of this phenomenon.

However, when we turn to the functional meaning of typology, we immediately see that Aalto defined this with extraordinary power, but given a very personal re-interpretation. Dominant examples include his apartment blocks, libraries, town halls, and theatres.

The Greek architect Demetri Porphyrios has sought to decipher the typological content of Aalto's plans and forms through the use of the concept **heterotopaeia**, to show that apparently unrelated elements of the buildings can be understood as fragments of wholes – which themselves, are in turn, in a proper relation to each other. Through this approach, he seeks to demonstrate that Aalto is best understood as a condenser of the European architectural tradition. But I do think it important to mention that, in so far as Aalto makes reference to types by composition, he 'dissolves' the Type in favour of the Site; he is interested in a Theory of Sites rather than a Theory of Types. It is a destruction of one of the longest-lived concepts of stability in building design.

Syntheses of tradition

The American scholar David Pearson has admirably documented the early phases of Aalto's career and shown how Aalto synthesized not only the informing traditions of Finnish architectural education of his time – what are known as National Romantic and Scandinavian Neo-Classical – but also rapidly absorbed lessons from the Classical architecture of the Mediterranean, from Art Nouveau (Jugendstil), from Russian Constructivism, from Scandinavian and Dutch Functionalism, and from the whole programme of Modernism in 20th century building. Moreover, Porphyrios has rightly commented that there is a strong element of **bricolage** in Aalto's work, of creating buildings from fragments drawn from uncoordinated and otherwise unrelated sources.

Curiously, although Aalto is enormously eclectic in his sources and influences, he does not display pastiche in any one building. We are not able to recognize obvious visual references to other styles. This is one of the greatest surprises in the work. Each building is coherent in its own terms, founded in his enduring analysis of the site, the function of the building and the ways in which human beings experience the world. The expressive systems used are not self-referential. We are not presented with an early version of 'Post-Modernism' (whatever that means in relation to buildings).

There is little to be gained from demonstrating that Aalto met this or that particular architect shortly before certain ideas appear in his work. The important question is what use he makes of what he borrows. We find rather a preoccupation with transforms, with making something new out of familiar material, which can be related directly to the role of experiment in his work. Precedents and other borrowings become somewhat like the grain of sand in the oyster – the basis of something altogether different.

The continuous experiment

The possibility occurs to one that such a small country as Finland could be used as a kind of laboratory to produce on a small scale things that the larger nations cannot make in their giant laboratories.

Alvar Aalto

211

Many of the buildings and larger plans designed in the Aalto office contain elements of earlier schemes; all schemes were subject to continuous adaptation. In itself, there is nothing unique about this. As suggested above, Mies van der Rohe's work can be understood as a series of distinct experimental conditions, of different combinations of structure, envelope, material, etc. However, we also find that Aalto would completely redesign whole schemes, even after they had been accepted.

We find that Aalto is encyclopedic in the range of architectural conditions he treats on an experimental basis. He had as his clients an extraordinary mixture: private individuals and large corporations, the church and the Communist Party, local communities and religious orders, universities and the Civil Guard, for central and local government. He designed small, medium and large buildings in cities, in towns, in suburbs and in the country. He designed for individual life and for communal life, although the latter was often nascent in the former. He designed houses, apartments, shops, offices, theatres and concert halls, libraries, galleries and museums, town halls, medical centres, hospitals, factories, educational buildings.

In each of these functional types, we can discover a transformational approach stemming from an analysis of what is the human experience of that activity.

The site and the route

> In modern architecture, where the rationality of the structural frame and the building masses threaten to dominate, there is often an architectural vacuum in the left-over portions of the site. It would be good if instead of filling this vacuum with decorative gardens the organic movement of people could be incorporated in the shaping of the site in order to create an intimate relationship between Man and Architecture.
>
> *Alvar Aalto*

The understanding of the **site** – its morphology, dimension, orientation and relationship to the surrounding area and infrastructure – is one of the crucial aspects in Aalto's work.

Aalto possessed a phenomenal ability to hold in his mind not just the form of the site, but its exact dimensions and geometry. On one notable occasion in the office (reported by a former assistant), he sat down at the drawing board and accurately reconstructed freehand from memory the whole site plan of his urban design for Lake Töölö and its surroundings, including some twenty buildings of varying size and shape, in a matter of hours.

Closely associated with the site are three considerations of **route**. The first is the path of the sun around the site/building; this defines the site/building in space and time. The second is the route of a human observer around the building – the 'reading' of the site – including external courtyards (a favourite device of Aalto's), which are never totally surrounded by building but remain in contact with the rest of the site. The third is the functional route of the person through the building, fulfilling the activities for which it has been designed.

This latter route is one of the means by which the buildings are given an experiential continuity of space: the buildings unfold as the person engages with the successive stages of function. He does not seek that continuity of interior and exterior space which often characterized modern buildings of his period. It would appear that, for Aalto, 'function' must be understood in terms of human experience.

Each building may then be interpreted, in the first instance, as a mediation between these three routes, between light – standing for Nature – site and function. As a result, we find that openings in vertical and horizontal enclosure – entrances, windows, internal courtyards and staircases – are often the physical forms by which this mediation is achieved in practice. After his youthful – and delightful – Neo-classical buildings of the early 1920s, Aalto generally eschewed the use of conventional architectural composition. He did not define approaches, entrances or routes by means of axes, symmetries, etc.; yet his buildings remain comprehensible, perhaps strange but not mysterious, a tacit but firm refutation of the premise that architecture has always to be defined in terms of the visually familiar.

A further refinement may be proposed here. The historian George Baird has drawn to our attention the importance of public space in Aalto's work, space which is accessible to the general public without having to be on business in that building. Baird tries to show how this can be used to understand the courtyards

Figure 32   Rautatalo, Helsinki, Finland ('The Iron House'): office building designed by Alvar Aalto. The interior shows the public atrium space.
The rooflights admit natural light; they have artificial lights outside, to
replace the natural lighting pattern in Winter or at night.

214

Figure 33 Enso-Gutzeit Headquarters, Helsinki, Finland: office building designed by Alvar Aalto. Note the external 'hollowing out' of the building's volume, to admit light to all parts of the building, and the complex array of screening devices on the windows.

(internal and external) which are such a frequent characteristic of Aalto's designs.

However, I suggest rather that these should be understood as an attempt to record and rehearse 'memory' of the site. That is, the physical organization, materials, decoration, etc. somehow conjure what the site was like before the building was constructed there. This comes strongly to mind when we see, first, how the surrounding surfaces are treated in their material and geometry, and secondly, the use of devices such as grass steps – e.g. at Seinäjoki town centre, the famous example at Säynätsalo, and so on. If we look in detail at different courtyards in Aalto's buildings, we may read the site as originally urban (e.g. Rautatalo, Fig. 32, or the Enzo-Gutzeit Headquarters, Fig. 33), or suburban (e.g. the Seinäjoki Town Hall and Parish Centre, Figs 34 and 35) or rural (e.g. Säynätsalo, Fig. 36). This significance of the courtyard, or 'atrium' if we use a more recent description, is strongly linked to Aalto's use of light, to which I now turn.

Figure 34 Town Centre, Seinäjoki, Finland: 'citizen's square' – a complex of civic buildings designed by Alvar Aalto. Note that there is no attempt to design them according to one visual style. Photo: Studio Kalevi A. Mäkinein.

Figure 35 Detail of the Town Hall, Seinäjoki, part of the citizen's square. Note the grass steps, evoking the suburban site which existed before the town centre was developed.

The use of light, the control of flows

A number of authors have remarked on the crucial role of light in Aalto's work and on his mastery of its manipulation.

It can be suggested that Aalto's 1924 trip to the Mediterranean awakened his interest in the visual modelling effects of strong sunlight. Much of his work can be understood as an attempt to evoke those Mediterranean qualities in a Nordic architecture.

One of the functions of the 'atrium', of the courtyards and other means by which the building volume is sculpted, is to bring light to all parts of the plan. For Aalto, windows are principally devices for bringing in light rather than for views to the surroundings. We can judge this in the Finlandiatalo, where the principal

217

Figure 36 Town Centre, Säynätsalo, Finland: a single construction involving all the civic elements for a small town – Council Chamber, library, medical centre, local authority offices, etc. Note the famous grass steps, literalizing the contour and, with the other vegetation in the courtyard, creating a memory of the rural site which existed before this construction. Photo: Eino Mäkinen, courtesy the Museum of Finnish Architecture, Helsinki.

and spectacular view – down Lake Töölö – is effectively blocked off (Figs 37 and 38). Light is never allowed to fall unconditioned: it is always baffled, reflected, mediated. This idea applies equally to the extraordinary array of artificial light fittings which Aalto designed over the years.

Light is used in the definition of the routes to which I referred above. For instance, because of the construction detail, windows may be screened from certain views, but become transparent as the observer moves around the building and/or the sun moves

Figure 37 Finlandiatalo, Helsinki, Finland: concert halls and conference centre, on Lake Töölö near the city centre, designed by Alvar Aalto.

Figure 38 View of Finlandiatalo from the other end of the Lake Töölö, the obvious 'view' to which we might expect the building to be oriented. The photograph shows how little the windows are turned this way: in Aalto's designs, windows are for admitting light into the building, rather than for giving views to the surroundings.

219

Figure 39 House, Jyväskylä, Finland: designed by Alvar Aalto. Note the timber detail – cover batten over vertical butt-joints, giving a 'corduroy' or 'reversed fluting' effect.

Figure 40 Detail of house (Fig. 39), showing timber battens over vertical butt-joints.

Figure 41 Alvar Aalto Museum, Jyväskylä, Finland: designed by Alvar Aalto. Note the 'reversed fluting' effect of the half-round vertical tiling on the walls.

Figure 42 Wall details of the Alvar Aalto Museum: note the 'reversed fluting' effect of the half-round vertical tiling on the walls, and its mixture with vertical timber battens over the windows. These are surface treatments, creating an ambiguity of the wall plane; they do not serve as sun screens or security devices.

221

Figure 43 Library at Rovaniemi, Finland: designed by Alvar Aalto. Note the vertical tiling on the walls and the painted steel grillage over the main window by the entrance. As one moves around the building, and/ or the sun moves around through the day, these screened windows appear and disappear – blending with the tiling, creating an ambiguity of surface and openings.

Figure 44 Drawings by Alvar Aalto to demonstrate his principle of directed but shadowless light, as part of the design of the library in Viipuri, Finland (now Vyborg, formerly USSR). This focus of the design on the experience and work of the functioning person is central to Aalto's approach – a humane functionalism. In this instance, function is defined through the relationship of light to the act of reading. Photo courtesy of Museum of Finnish Architecture.

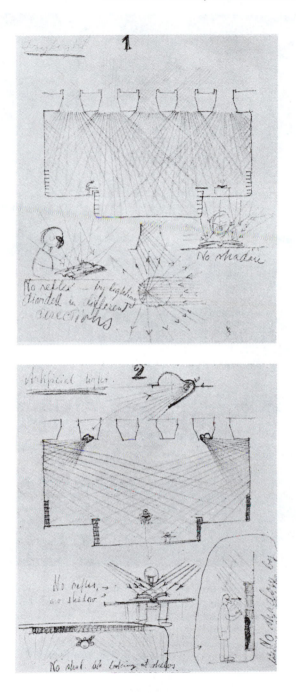

Figure 45 The Sanatorium at Paimio, Finland: designed by Alvar Aalto. Originally a tuberculosis clinic, seeking sunlight and pine forest air as the only means of cure at the time (early 1930s). The discovery/invention of penicillin made the building obsolete and it became a general hospital. Its form is that of a sunflower – the functional spaces are arranged according to their relationship to the sun. The south-facing ward block is shown here.

around the site: the changing eye and the changing light source equally animate the building.

One of the forms of this animation is to introduce an ambiguity into the definition of the building volume. Many of his surfaces display a vertical 'reverse fluting' or 'corduroy effect' (Figs 39–43). As with the fluting of the Classical column, recalled briefly in some of the details on Aalto's office in Helsinki, the movement of sunlight across the surface causes the exact surface to shimmer. This particular detail is also used in the successive occlusion/ transparency already described for windows.

When we examine Aalto's drawings and other representations, we discover that he uses optical geometry for the study of sound (Fig. 44), ray diagrams for plans, for the flow of water, and so on. I am driven to the conclusion that, for Aalto, light stands for Nature – it is a metonym, a representative symbol (as the Crown in Britain stands for the whole apparatus of royalty). The control of light is in fact the control of Nature. I believe that this conception arose from his early functional analyses of buildings in which light – and particularly sunlight – was crucial to the very idea of the building.

The two critical examples are the Viipuri Library, in which light is essential to the act of reading, and the Paimio Sanatorium, in which sunlight was essential to the healing of tuberculosis (for which the Sanatorium was originally designed, before the discovery of penicillin).

The Paimio hospital (Fig. 45) is set in a pine forest – another element of Nature – which became part of its function, the healing process. It is absorbed into his architecture and planning, but is also often evoked in the striated light which results from the details I have identified above. I conclude that Aalto displayed opposites and divergences in part to demonstrate that their architectural resolution was, in some sense, a healing mediation: as in physical elements, so in social elements.

The use of materials

The first essential feature is Karelian architecture's uniformity . . . in which timber dominates . . . in most cases naked, without the dematerialising effect that a layer of paint gives. A Karelian village is somehow similar in appearance to a Greek ruin . . .

Alvar Aalto

225

Baird, and following him, another historian, Wrede, have argued that Aalto used particular materials because he sought to evoke 'the ruin' in his work. For Baird, this is because Aalto was appalled at the rapid ravages of time on his buildings, with its modern details, and tried to pre-empt its worst effects. For Wrede, this use of materials and ruined forms is more part of an argument that archaeology plays a major role in Aalto's scheme of things. I consider that this attributes to Aalto too great a preoccupation with retaining the past, whereas I argue that he transforms elements from the past into forms for contemporary life. The physical erosion of the building geometry is partly a pragmatic means of bringing light into critical parts of the plan, and partly an expression again of what is characterized above as a Theory of Sites which dissolves the Type.

As with functional types, so with materials. Aalto uses virtually every building material we have – reinforced concrete, brick, timber (almost a new material in his hands), stucco, copper, bronze, marble, granite, terracotta, glass, ceramics. The only major building material we do not find used to any great extent is structural steelwork or steel cladding. Colour is never applied to the materials on Aalto's buildings: paint is either black or white; other colours derive from the materials themselves (e.g. strongly coloured ceramic tiles). 'Dematerialization' – the trick by which the solidity of the building apparently dissolves into a shimmer – is accomplished by light and geometry. The concepts of plane and solid are destabilized, notably by screen effects.

Although he had a good traditional understanding of how building materials behaved, these materials are rarely used by Aalto simply for their intrinsic physical properties, but rather for their compositional and geometric qualities. The development of the screens, described above, is one powerful version of how Aalto treats a great variety of materials: these screens both depict his interest in composition of line, plane, etc., and also by a complex layering of the surface continue the deconstruction of the Type by assisting the ambiguity of form already begun by the dynamic behaviour of light on these surfaces: light unites with material in animating site and function.

The natural order and the rational order

The most straightforward account of Aalto's underlying programme of design is that he seeks to place architecture and
planning at the opposition between Man and Nature, between

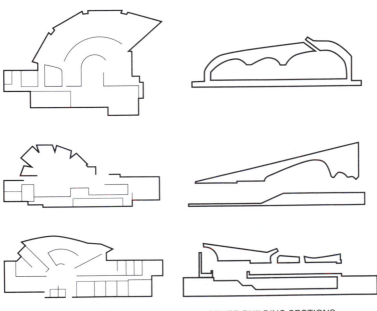

LIBRARY PLANS   OTHER BUILDING SECTIONS

Figure 46   An ideogram (top) suggested by Professor Wilson of Cambridge University. It presents the horizon and the sky, the natural and
the rational. Its form also relates to typical plan and section conditions of
Aalto designs, as the other schematic drawings (from Aalto's designs)
indicate.

227

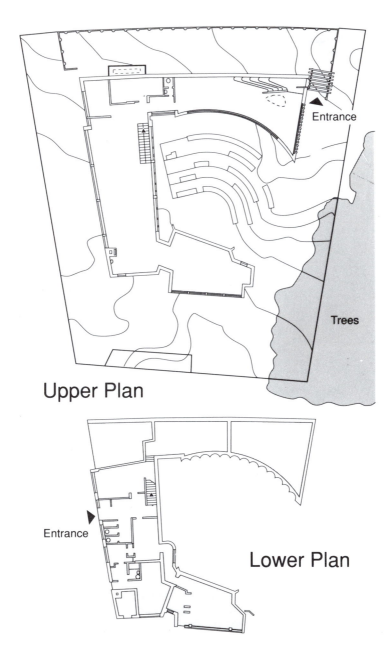

Upper Plan

Lower Plan

the rational order and the natural order. This is of course a classic programme for architecture, but it is in Aalto that we find it expressed so vigorously, and in such profusion, and through a functionalist analysis of human experience.

Light is taken to stand for Nature and its control is the control of Nature. Sunlight is the animated form of natural light: by controlling and mediating that sunlight, life is brought into the building. The use of ray diagrams in a wide range of drawings – to stand for light, for sound and for many other behaviours – is the practical design version of this proposition. Aalto is preoccupied with this fundamental flow of Nature and its relationship to the flow of space in and around buildings.

Equally, the site is best understood by the experience of humans moving across and around it. It is a dynamic element, not an archaeological remnant, and creates a tension for anyone there – with the dynamic of light and the dynamic of function.

These ideas are effectively summarized in an ideogram (Fig. 46) proposed by the English architect Colin St John Wilson, the combination of the straight line and the wavy line, which evokes the physical forms of so many Aalto plans and volumes. I think it can stand for horizon and sky, natural and man-made (artificial?), free-form and regular, both/and, stasis and flux.

The clearest example of this proposition is the Aalto office in Helsinki (Fig. 47), where the 'gradient' of the building passes from the right-angle of the street to the natural order of the forest fragment.

The Aalto Atelier

A more detailed analysis can be proposed for the 1956 atelier (see plan in Fig. 48, marked A–M), which is one of the Aalto

---

Figure 47 The Aalto Atelier, Helsinki, Finland: architect's office for himself, designed by Alvar Aalto, on a suburban site. The site slopes down from the road and one enters at the lower level. There is a secondary entrance direct to Aalto's own work space. The stair to the upper level takes one to the main office and to Aalto's own work space (which looks down the garden through the curved wall). The garden is an amphitheatre, formed by the walls and by literalizing the natural contours of the ground.

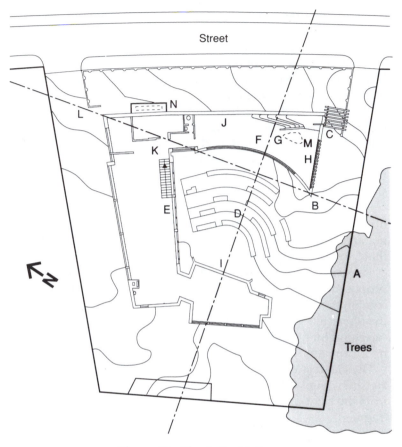

Figure 48   The Aalto Atelier.

masterworks, a building in which we can find almost all of Aalto's architectural preoccupations developed with clarity and rigour, but with the lightest of touches. The plan repays detailed analysis.

The flow of space from the forest fragment (A) divides either side of the 'prow' of the building (B) (Fig. 49), one part to the master entrance (C), the other through the south-facing amphitheatre, a formalization (D) of the contours (Figs 50 and 51) which also encapsulates the ideas in his various grass-stepped courtyards – e.g. at Säynätsalo, Seinäjoki Town Hall and Parish Centre – memories of the sites before the buildings came. The spatial flow here also represents the potential movement of people

Figure 49 The great curved wall of the atelier, rising to a 'prow' Photo: Heikki Havas, courtesy the Museum of Finnish Architecture.

Figure 50 The amphitheatre of the garden, made by literalizing the contours. Note the window to the main studio on the upper floor.

Figure 51 The amphitheatre of the garden, made by literalizing the contours. Note door at right, at the 'knuckle' of the plan, leading from the top of the stairs into the garden.

around the site. It is balked at the wall to the main drawing office (E); this has its counterpoint in the flow of space (Fig. 52) through the master studio (F), which divides to the interior of the master door (C), around the freestanding wall (G) – lit by the rooflight overhead (M) – and which is also balked at the high end-wall (H). In both cases, the high-level clerestory windows reinforce the termination of space and the blocking of the pedestrian routes. These two flows sweep either side of the great curved wall.

From the blank wall (I), which with the curved wall formally identifies the axis of the amphitheatre (D), the space also steps up the contours and 'through' the low window in the curved wall to balk at the blank back wall (J): this appears to be one of the few – if not the only – windows in Aalto's buildings to demonstrate a Modern Movement precept about the continuity of internal and external space and to give deliberate views to the exterior. (Usually we find in Aalto's designs that windows exist to bring light into the buildings, not to give views outwards.)

Part of these spatial flows may be seen to crash against the wall (G), up through the overhead rooflight, and against the back of the small room (M), through another small rooflight (N). These two rooflights somehow lock the position of the main street wall (J), much in the fashion of the internal and external staircase on the

Figure 52 Aalto's own work space. Note the secondary entrance, the high window (at right) and the rooflight in front of the short, free-standing wall. Photo: Leonardo Mosso, courtesy the Museum of Finnish Architecture.

long wall of the Finlandia Hall (Fig. 53), in order then to set it adrift in ambiguities about its location through surface treatment and 'dematerialization'.

The plan pivots around a 'knuckle' (K), where the doors make the transition between interior and exterior and where the stair joins upper and lower levels on the north element of the building. That is, it is the crossing-point of the various routes around and through the building. The amphitheatre makes plain the memory of the site, which in this instance illustrates the pre-conditions of a Garden City.

The building as a whole demonstrates in almost programmatic terms Aalto's concern to use architecture as the mediation be-tween the natural and the man-made worlds. We can draw a gradient line from the (nearly) right-angle of the street pattern (L), through the knuckle (K) to the forest (A).

Figure 53 Finlandiatalo, Helsinki, Finland: detail of the concert hall complex, showing articulated and enclosed stairs, which together define the wall plane, and which in turn is then given ambiguity by the play of light on the fluted surface.

This gradient is virtually perpendicular to the amphitheatre axis, and together these form the matrix of spatial complexity in the whole building: the mediating function can be read along the gradient either way. One gradient leads North from the natural to the rational world; the other takes us from the most impenetrable (enclosing) wall through a series of screens to the street. The two axes also acknowledge the movement of the sun during the day. Their combination defines the system of routes for people within and around the building. It may also be apparent that the systems of walls/planes comprise sets of rays generated from points outside the site.

The only free-form element, the great curving wall rising to its 'prow', is also the only wall which is permeable to space: this ambivalence is reinforced by the treatment of the wall beneath the long window, which has a clear reference to the fluting of classical columns, a motif which I have argued elsewhere is at the root of Aalto's conception of the dematerialized wall. The Classical reference is, of course, explicit in the evocation of the Greek theatre embedded in the hillside.

At an everyday level, the building is light and airy, quiet because it turns its back on the street, calm and organized. Whether full of people or virtually empty, the scale is always appropriate because of the articulation of the plan into smaller semi-volumes. Moreover, whilst in and around the building, one is not conscious of the highly abstract ordering of the space in any formalistic way, rather one feels the quiet dynamic as an animation of site, light, space and structure which supports work and repose.

This specific analysis indicates the complexity and abstraction of Aalto's conception of space as a particular set of flows, notably of light (which also stands for Nature) and people. It touches on their implications for the treatment of materials and building elements. The examination of the functional route shows it to be the operator which breaks down traditional types into specific solutions for specific sites.

The precursor of today

> When, during the late-medieval flowering, the cathedral raised itself in every city above the insignificant build-ings' tight confusion, it was a symbol for life's difficult unity.
>
> *Alvar Aalto*

As will be apparent from the language used in presenting my interpretation of Aalto's planning and architecture, I see the work from his office as the crucial precursor of more recent theoretical preoccupations. Some of these preoccupations have arisen in theoretical writings of architecture; others have emerged in build-ing science, as investigators have begun to make explicit the complexities of how people perceive, enjoy and respond to the environments of buildings.

In many ways, Aalto's buildings can be read as built criticism of a variety of current positions and critical viewpoints in architecture/ building today.

In the critical writing about Aalto's work, and his designs have

235

been a potent source of ideas for designers and builders ever since he presented them, some have argued that he was a simple soul who stumbled through 'Modern Architecture' and emerged to show a more humane way of designing. I deny that Aalto was some sort of homespun philosopher who sought to set aside ideas from the Modern Movement or who was, in some sense, indifferent or unknowing of abstract ideas.

On the contrary, I suggest that of all the major proponents of 20th century architecture in Europe and North America, Aalto operated at the most abstract level. He was a highly cultivated man, steeped in European culture.

He denied any special role for theory in his work. This does not mean that we cannot validly point to an enduring and coherent theoretical programme in the work. The regularities and pre-occupations are so crucial to the experience of the buildings that they must be confronted for an explanation. Any such explanation should acknowledge the ways in which he balanced holistic and reductionist factors, the ways in which he manipulated the flows of the physical world in an extraordinary and abstract fashion to design buildings which are beautiful, comfortable, distinct, humane, of our time, unassuming and – somehow – both rich and straightforward.

Further reading

Baird, G. and Futogawa, Y. (1970) *Alvar Aalto*, Thames & Hudson, London.

Blaser, W. (1985) *Atrium: 5000 years of Open Courtyards*, Welf & Co. AG Verlag, Basel.

Groák, S. (1978) Notes on responding to Aalto's buildings. *Architectural Monographs*, No. 4: Alvar Aalto, Academy Editions, London.

Mosso, L. (1960) La luce nell'architettura di Alvar Aalto. *Zodiac*, 7, 66–115.

Pearson, P.D. (1978) *Alvar Aalto and the International Style*, Whitney Library of Design, New York.

Pearson, P.D. (1979) The legacy of Viipuri. *Architectural Design*, **49**(12), 6–13.

Porphyrios, D. (1982) *Sources of Modern Eclecticism*, Academy Editions, London.

Rautsi, J. (1986) Alvar Aalto's urban plans, 1940–70. *RIBA Transactions 9*, **5**, 48–61.

Wilson, C.St J. (1981) Alvar Aalto and the state of Modernism, in *Alvar Aalto vs the Modern Movement* (ed. K. Mikkola), Rakennuskirjo Oy, Helsinki.

INCONCLUSION

Consider the essentials of the door: its use (the 'dynamic') and its non-use (the 'static').

The dynamic situation
Should one wish to enter or to leave some room in question, then in either case the door itself is entirely superfluous. The sole necessity is an opening, a door-frame of standard measurement.

The static situation
Should one wish to remain either inside or outside the room, then equally a door is unnecessary. Here our need is an attractive but solid wall, also of standard measurement.

Thus we see that in our simple model there is no necessity for the door at all.

However, as with many simple models, reality may be a complex combination of our basic situations. Let us consider certain hybrids, before we accept conclusions.

The dyna-static situation
Here we have the room bounded only by the sturdy wall, unperforated. But we wish either to enter or to leave this room.

The stati-dynamic situation
This is the room with door-frames constructed on sound principle. However, here we wish neither to enter nor to leave; we accept our present condition.

In both of these latter situations, the answers deduced from the simple model were unsatisfactory. Both wall and frame, in the wrong place, are inadequate.

In conclusion, then, we see that the door is a useful compromise leading to mental comfort. This is a relief.

Author index

Subject index